Death by Church
Life Through Christ

Hope for the Hopeless

Death by Church
Life Through Christ

Hope for the Hopeless

Mike Lee

ABOOKS
Alive Book Publishing

Death by Church
Life Through Christ
Hope for the Hopeless
Copyright © 2022 by Mike Lee

Additional copies may be ordered from the publisher for educational,
business, promotional or premium use.
For information, contact ALIVE Book Publishing at:
alivebookpublishing.com, or call (925) 837-7303.

Book Design by Alex Johnson
Quotes from the Bible are from the New International Version (NIV).

ISBN 13
978-1-63132-184-9

Library of Congress Control Number: 2022921018

Library of Congress Cataloging-in-Publication Data
is available upon request.

First Edition

Published in the United States of America by ALIVE Book Publishing
and ALIVE Publishing Group, imprints of Advanced Publishing LLC
3200 A Danville Blvd., Suite 204, Alamo, California 94507
alivebookpublishing.com

PRINTED IN THE UNITED STATES OF AMERICA

10 9 8 7 6 5 4 3 2 1

Foreword

Have you ever blown it big time? Have you ever had the thing you wanted in the palm of your hand and you knew you were about to drop it, but you just couldn't stop yourself from letting go? Did you play the scenario forward and see that train wreck in your future? Did you buy the lie that bad consequences happen only to other people? I think many of us have. I know I have. Mike Lee has, and in *Death by Church* he explores issues close to our hearts with a determined boldness and raw honesty. He walks us through the biblical truths of sin, forgiveness and moving forward. He helps us understand why and how to make peace with our missteps. He causes us to examine our treatment of fellow sinners in our relationships and in our churches, and learn to show love. He gives us hope that God will free us from the chains of our sins and use our messes to build His Kingdom. Throughout history, God has reclaimed the most imperfect people to act on His behalf. Mike says, "There's hardly a man or woman in the Bible used greatly by God who didn't fail greatly."

I first met Mike over a decade ago when God led my family to what is now Mike's former church. Friends had been going there and told us that something special was going on; they said we needed to hear the pastor speak. We found that God had anointed Mike, giving him an ability to relay insightful perceptions of biblical truths delivered in an easy conversational style. Mike doesn't talk at you or preach booming from the pulpit, he speaks to you like you're sitting at a table in a café—or these days, in a bar at Rey's Restaurant—and rapping about God. This book is written in that same relaxed tone: you're sitting down with a wise friend who's imparting some godly life facts that just might change your life…if you allow it. It's this coffee-talk ease that attracted the Raleigh, North Carolina area masses to form one of the largest churches in the country. They came to listen to Mike. They came for Mike because he made God's Word understandable and relatable. His decades of solid Bible study partnered with a theological degree and a humility to seek counsel, other expert input and, most of all, God's mighty direction ensured the accuracy of those messages which were heard by tens of thousands of pairs of eager ears every week. And you are lucky, because through this book you can also partake of that wellspring of teaching which has the power to alter your life in positive and beneficial ways.

Mike's first book, *You Can't God Can: Making a Difference in Your World,* teaches us how big of a deal it is to God for us to influence others' spiritual lives. "There will be more rejoicing in heaven over one sinner who repents than over ninety-nine righteous persons who do not need to repent" (Luke 15:7 NIV). Partnering symmetrically with that message of sharing the Good News with others, in these pages Mike speaks to the concept of biblical restoration in relation to ourselves, to others and to our church entities. "Brothers and sisters, if someone is caught in a sin, you who live by the Spirit should restore that person gently" (Galatians 6:1 NIV).

Whoever has hurt you, whether a church body, a fellow Christian or other person, or whether you suffer from the effects of your own actions, *Death by Church* is a salve for your wounds. When I first read this book, it affected me in the most profound and helpful way, and it was a totally God-directed experience. Mike had approached me to edit an early draft of this book at a time when I was juggling a lot emotionally. My husband of twenty years had recently died and I was struggling with some things from my past while trying to help my college-aged kids figure out their futures without their dad's counsel. I wasn't sure I could handle the project. But it was Mike. And God had me typing a hasty "yes!" in an email before I had even had time to think it through. I work as an editor and writer/author, having written and published a few books myself, so the editing job was in line with my God-given talents. As I read the stories and teachings in this book, it literally healed years of regret and shame from my past brought on by my own actions. It helped me to shine light on the darkest parts of my history and allowed God to heal the hurt that lived there. It set my future steps joyfully and firmly aligned in freedom with God's guidance. Will I stumble again? *Definitely.* Will I break free from the bonds of my sin and walk in the freedom of Christ? *Definitely.* As Mike says, "When I am at my worst, God is at His best."

I know for a fact that if you read this book and allow the words to speak to your hurt and your heart, you will begin to find the freedom God wants you experience for yourself and others. My prayer for you is that you allow God to speak to you through this teaching and open your eyes and mind to the concept of forgiveness as God intends, learning to love others so that you can proceed to do great things for the Kingdom.

~ Catherine Anne Lewis
Co-author, *Bittersweet: Faith Lost and Found,*
and *The DNA Test that Brought a Baby Back to Life*
catherineannelewis.com

Chapter 1

"Welcome to My Sh*t Show!"

We had a saying, "Hang around the pond long enough and you might fall in!" It began in 1994, after years of pastoring in California, when our family relocated along with four other families to North Carolina to start a church. Over a period of twenty-seven years, by God's grace, the church grew from that small core to one of the largest churches in America. It was an incredible place where the broken and downcast were accepted and loved. It was a shelter in the storm for those whose lives were falling apart. It was a safe place to sit and listen and ponder the gospel message. It was a pond where people fell in. Many who attend the church today would attest, "That's my story." It was a place that exemplified grace and mercy and second chances. It was a place of incredible unity, in fact, there were only seven "no" votes in over twenty-five years of church business meetings. Compare that to the average church! In fact, there's an old saying, "Wherever two or three Baptists are gathered in Jesus' name, there will be at least four opinions." That wasn't this church. There was unheard of unity. It was also a church of impact, not only in our community, but around the world.

During my years of ministry I experienced God's faithfulness time and time again. I served as a pastor for forty years and I never experienced a year when the church that I led decreased in attendance. In spite of financial crises and tough times, I never once had to layoff an employee because of a shortage of funds. I was blessed and I knew it. I sat back and watched as God worked in the hearts of individuals who didn't even attend our church as He moved them to give us property to build campuses. I enjoyed the ride as I had a front row seat to witness God change the hearts of city council members so that said property could be rezoned and developed to advance His Kingdom. I would love to take credit for what transpired during those twenty-seven years, but to be totally honest, I had no idea what I was doing and I have no problem admitting that.

When the church reached an attendance of 2,000, I fought major depression because I had zero desire to pastor a large church. I had no idea how to lead it forward, and as the church continued to grow, I found myself hanging on for dear life. It was like trying to ride a wild stallion without a saddle or reins. I had no choice other than to trust and follow God. I never relied on business books or the latest strategies. I avoided conferences like the plague. I still don't know what an "EOS" is. The only rocks I'd ever moved were in my yard. Things like "risk management" weren't a part of my strategy as I contemplated where God was leading us, because I could never quite figure out how to balance risk management and faith. I didn't really care what other, more successful churches were doing; I trusted God to do what only He could do. He led and I followed. I had been in ministry long enough to know that, as a leader, I had very little to do with the church's success. I knew that for some reason God had chosen to place His hand of blessing on us, and I also knew that He could remove his blessing anytime He saw fit. I worked hard seven days a week and I loved it...99% of the time. It wasn't a job; it was an adventure that I never wanted to end. I never planned to retire. I had every intention of staying on that wild stallion until the day I died. In fact, I used to joke with the congregation that my desire was to preach my final message and then just drop dead, have a quick funeral since everyone was already present, and then everyone go to lunch and have a martini. That was my "happily-ever-after" dream.

In forty years of ministry, I took pride in the fact that I had never taken a sabbatical. One of my closest and wisest friends on staff had started to see some cracks in my life and he encouraged me on a regular basis to take some time off and get away. I told him that I thought it sent a bad message to the congregation. I joked that sabbaticals were for Millennials (not totally a joke). After all, God was supposed to be my refuge and source of strength, and so I just plowed ahead...and eventually it caught up with me.

One morning I woke up at 4am, and as I sat in my living room in the dark I realized that something inside of me was broken. I felt numb and void of emotions. I felt that I was experiencing some level of a breakdown. A few days later, I bared my soul to my board and asked for something that I had never asked for in forty years; I asked for some time off to get healthy. Unfortunately, we were just entering into the time of COVID with racial unrest, social uncertainty and unprecedented fear, and those in leadership felt that the timing just wasn't right. Knowing what I know now, I wish I had pushed back harder and demanded a break; that's on me. I also wish that my board would have been more sensitive to my situation, and looking back, I'm sure they would now agree. But I truly believe that everyone was doing the best they could under some extreme circumstances. And since I had a twenty-seven year track record of navigating through tough times, I did what I was expected to do and what I had always done. Even though I was exhausted and running on empty, I put my head down and I plowed through for ten more months. I did my job. My board even praised me later for preaching some of my best sermons during that time period. But on the inside I was a dead man walking. I had lost all of my joy. I was spiritually 'on empty'. I felt angry, resentful and unappreciated, but I bottled up my feelings and kept everything to myself. Instead of running to God and finding my strength in Him, I isolated myself more and more. Looking back now, the parallels between Elijah hiding inside a cave and me hiding inside my office were eerily similar. No one knew what I was going through; I wasn't even aware of what I was going through. But I did know that the church I loved and that had given me so much joy was killing me. Like many other pastors who realize it too late, I realized that I was experiencing death by church.

And then the unthinkable happened; I had a moral failure. But as I begin this book, I want to make it clear that I am in no way justifying or excusing my actions. No one held a gun to my head and forced me to do what I did; I am 100% responsible. And at the writing of this book, I would love to say that my life has returned to normal and that all is well, but I'm still on the journey; I am still in the healing process and there are days when it feels like I'm making little to no progress. It's three steps forward and two steps back. My world has been turned upside down and all of the repentance, confession and counseling in the world will not magically fix all that has been broken. Trust me, I know. Consequences are consequences and they have to be dealt with.

I feel like David must have felt when he realized that things weren't going to work out the way he thought they were going to work out in his life. Have you ever experienced that? Have you discovered that sometimes our plans don't go as we expect them to go, and sometimes it's funny, but sometimes it's not? For example, you can look back and laugh when your GPS leads you to a destination other than the one you desired, but then you ended up having a better time at your unplanned stop than you would have had if you had made it to your original destination. You can look back on a situation like that as a fond memory and laugh.

But it's not all that funny when you have a dream for your life and then you wake up one day and realize, "The hope and dream I had for my life isn't going to happen. In fact, not only is it not going to happen, it can't happen." And when we come to one of those moments where it seems as if life is spinning out of control and we lose our bearings, it's because that thing we've always hoped and planned our life around is out of reach. It's when you and your spouse realize your happily-ever-after isn't going to happen. It's when you realize during the engagement that your wedding isn't going to happen. It's when you discover that you're not going to have children. It's when you realize that you're going to have to shut down the business you've invested your entire life in. It's when you realize that you're not going to get into the school you've always dreamed about attending. It's when the reality hits you that you're not going to finish the way you had always planned to finish. It when you realize that you've arrived a destination you never planned to arrive at. That's my story. As I stated earlier, my hope and dream was to finish my ministry at the church I started twenty-eight years ago, but now I realize that isn't going to happen; it can't happen. You've probably had a similar experience, too.

You can see this scenario in a little known, but fascinating story, from the life of David. In this story, we find David sitting on the back of a donkey, heading out of Jerusalem. And on the back of that donkey it hits him: "My dream isn't going to happen; it can't happen." And in the midst of what must have been overwhelming emotion and despair, there are some truths that come out of David's situation that will allow all of us to experience the grace of God in our lives, and maybe like never before when we come to the same realization that David did.

The story is found in 2 Samuel 15, but to appreciate the story, you have to know the background, and so I want to give you a decade of history that will only take you a couple minutes to read. One of the more well-known stories in David's life has to do with his affair with Bathsheba that led to the murder of Bathsheba's husband, Uriah. The whole thing was a big mess.

And if things weren't terrible enough as a result of the affair and murder, things went from bad to worse for David; in fact, his whole family fell completely apart. For example, David had been promised by God that one of his sons would follow him on the throne, and David naturally assumed that Amnon, his first-born son, would be his replacement. That was normal protocol in those days. But it just so happened that Amnon fell in love with his half-sister, Tamar, David's daughter from another marriage. And Amnon wanted her so badly that one day he faked being sick, and when Tamar brought him lunch, Amnon raped her. And when David hears about what happened, he doesn't do anything about it. But when Absalom, David's third-born son and Tamar's blood brother, hears about the rape, he's incredibly angry, but he's also incredibly patient. Absalom allows two years to go by until things settle down. And after waiting for two years, he plans a big dinner party and invites all his brothers and sisters, and at the party, in front of all his siblings, he kills Amnon and then Absalom flees the country. And when David hears about Amnon's murder, he's stuck between a rock and a hard place, because his firstborn son has been murdered by Absalom who's the apple of his father's eye, yet once again, David does nothing.

Three more years go by and David assumes that things have settled down, so he invites Absalom to come back to Jerusalem, and Absalom returns but David won't see him or talk to him. Two more years go by and David finally restores Absalom to his inner circle, and I'm sure that by restoring him he thought, "One day Absalom will sit on the throne and will be the king." And so he brings Absalom back to the palace, and for four years things seem to be working out. But what David doesn't realize is that Absalom still has all of this unresolved, pent up anger against him, and eventually Absalom begins to secretly recruit people to follow him. In fact, it says in 2 Samuel 15:5-6 (NIV): "Whenever anyone approached him to bow down before him, Absalom would reach out his hand, take hold of him and kiss him. Absalom behaved in this way toward all the Israelites who came to the king asking for justice, and so he stole the hearts of the people of Israel." And so even though people respected David, they loved Absalom, and so Absalom came up with a plan to take the throne from his dad that would require only one small skirmish.

The story continues in 2 Samuel 15:10-16: "Then Absalom sent secret messengers throughout the tribes of Israel to say, 'As soon as you hear the sound of the trumpets, then say, "Absalom is king in Hebron."' Two hundred men from Jerusalem had accompanied Absalom. They had been invited as guests and went quite innocently, knowing nothing about the matter. While Absalom was offering sacrifices, he also sent for Ahithophel the Gilonite, David's counselor, to come from Giloh, his hometown. And so the conspiracy gained strength, and Absalom's following kept on increasing. A messenger came and told David, 'The hearts of the people of Israel are with Absalom.' Then David said to all his officials who were with him in Jerusalem, 'Come! We must flee, or none of us will escape from Absalom. We must leave immediately, or he will move quickly to overtake us and bring ruin on us and put the city to the sword.' The king's officials answered him, 'Your servants are ready to do whatever our lord the king chooses.' The king set out, with his entire household following him; but he left ten concubines to take care of the palace."

And suddenly, riding out of town on the back of a donkey, David realizes that the future is nothing like he had dreamed or planned or anticipated; in fact, everything had gone wrong. And in that one afternoon, his hopes and dreams about how God would demonstrate faithfulness to him, disintegrate.

And David realizes, "There are no good options." He realizes that if he stays and fights, regardless of who wins, the city of Jerusalem will be destroyed. If he wages war with his own son, one of three things will happen: either David will be killed; or Absalom will be killed; or, they both will be killed. And even if

he captured Absalom alive, he'll face the reality of having to ex-
ecute his own son for treason. There are no good options.

So, David and his family scramble around and pack up all of
their valuables. They loaded up their mules and donkeys and
horses and they head out of town. And the people lined the
streets weeping as their once great king flees for his life from his
own son. And as David rides out of town, he has to be thinking,
"God, how did this happen? I'm at the place in life when I'm
supposed to be turning over the throne to Absalom. There's no
way that any good can come out of this." And in the midst of
this overwhelming situation, David gives us a truth that sheds
some insight into the ways of God. But before I show it to you,
I want to address something. Some of you can relate to David
and his emotions because you've also realized that your dreams
aren't going to come true. Your relationship isn't going to work
out. You're not going to get that job or that promotion. You're
not going to get into that school. Your kids aren't going to turn
out the way you thought they would turn out. And when we're
faced with that kind of hard, cold reality, after the sense of frustration and disappointment begins to fade, it's often followed
by anger. And we get so mad because life just isn't supposed to
be this way!

For example, maybe you've been saving yourself for the right
person, but now you're forty and you're still single and you're
like, "God, I don't want to stay single forever!" Or maybe you
wouldn't compromise your integrity when your boss asked you
to and as a result, you ended up losing your job and you are left
thinking, "What's the point?" Or, maybe you served in a role
and you gave it everything you had until you were at the point
of exhaustion; maybe even a breakdown. And you asked for a
break to catch your breath and get your feet back under you, but
your request was ignored. Maybe you were promised a retirement package for years of sacrificial service but it never materi-
alized. And you were left feeling like, "After all my faithfulness

and service and commitment, if this is the way God's going to reward me, I'm done. What's the point of being faithful and obedient if this is the payoff?"

But do you know what the tragedy is when we respond that way (and this is what I'm learning)? It still doesn't put our shattered world back together. It still doesn't restore what we've lost. It still doesn't heal the hurt. In fact, it just sends us down a road that ultimately results in more pain, more hurt and more consequences, plus it leaves us cynical, bitter and hard to live with. And it's somewhat understandable why we go down that road because we've lost our dream; we've lost what's important to us. And it's hard to maintain faith in a sovereign God who would allow that kind of thing to happen.

Fortunately for David, he'd been here before. Earlier in his life he had his issues with King Saul. And there was a time when David said, "God, if this is the best you can do, I'm taking control of my life." And he left Jerusalem and went to the city of Nob where he took matters into his own hands and it was a disaster. And now, years later, he's headed out of Jerusalem for the second time and he knows one thing for sure, "I'm not turning my back on God; I'm not losing hope; I'm not giving up on God because I've been there before and I know how that ended."

So, what does David do; how does he respond? 2 Samuel 15:23-24 says: "The whole countryside wept aloud as all the people passed by. The king also crossed the Kidron Valley, and all the people moved on toward the wilderness. Zadok was there, too, and all the Levites who were with him were carrying the Ark of the Covenant of God. They set down the ark of God, and Abiathar offered sacrifices until all the people had finished leaving the city."

By the way, this was during a time when the presence of God resided in a box called the Ark of the Covenant, and that means that everywhere the Ark went, God went, and that meant that whoever had the box was in good shape. For example, when you went into battle, you made sure you took God-in-the-box with you because if you had God-in-the-box, you won; God's presence was attached to that box. So, when David's guys are packing up to leave Jerusalem, they're thinking, "We're taking the box with us! We may leave our wives and kids, but we're not leaving the box because wherever the box goes, that's who wins."

So, they pick up the ark and start hauling it off. And as they're making their way out of Jerusalem, David stops and looks at the ark and it dawns on him what's about to happen. And he says, "Send the ark back to Jerusalem." And his entourage is like, "You're going to send God back to Jerusalem?" And I'm sure they were thinking, "Do you mind if we go with Him?" But David made the decision to send the ark back because he realized that he was about to attempt to manipulate the situation to regain control, because, after all, whoever had the box, wins. But all of a sudden it hits him, "That's not what this is about." And notice what David says in 2 Samuel 15:25-26: "Then the king said to Zadok, 'Take the ark of God back into the city. If I find favor in the Lord's eyes, He will bring me back and let me see it and His dwelling place again. But if He says, "I am not pleased with you," then I am ready; let Him do to me whatever seems good to Him.'"

And that's the key.

Now, I'm going to warn you, this is going to sound like an oversimplification of an answer to your specific issue, but this is the answer. David basically says, "God, here are my plans and hopes and dreams; this is what I assumed you wanted for my life; this is how I thought things would play out. You take these things and you do to me whatever you need to do; I'm sending the box back. I'm casting all my cares and hopes and dreams upon your providential grace." And if you read the rest of the story, you will discover that David's decision created the context for God to answer David's prayers and fulfill His promise to

David. And in making this decision, David avoided three mistakes we often make when we face the death of a dream.

First, David didn't attach his faith in God to the fulfillment of his dreams. In other words, it wasn't, "If my dreams go away, my faith in God goes away." He avoided that mistake.

Second, David didn't attach his faith in God to his assumptions about how God would fulfill his promise. Just like us, David had a promise from God, and just like us, David assumed he knew how God would fulfill the promise of placing his heir on the throne. He assumed it would be his firstborn, Amnon. And if that didn't work out for some reason, Absalom was waiting in the wings. But just because it didn't go down the way he assumed it would go down, David didn't lose faith in God's ability to fulfill the promise.

By the way, what is God's promise to you? God has promised to never leave you nor forsake you. But what does it look like? In most of our minds it means that we're going to be healthy and our kids are going to grow up healthy. It means that our marriage will stay together. It means that our kids will grow up and do all the things we envision them doing. It means we'll always have a fulfilling job and enough money. Those are the assumptions that most of us attach to God's promise, "I will never leave you or forsake you," but it's a huge mistake to assume that. Sure, we have ideas. Sure, we have a vision of the future. Sure, we have hopes and dreams, but David was wiser and older and he knew better. He didn't attach his faith in God to his assumptions about how God would fulfill His promise.

Third, David didn't take matters into his own hands and try to manipulate the situation. He looked at the ark and said, "Send it back, we'll trust God to sort it all out. And if God chooses to send me back to Jerusalem, so be it. And if God chooses to not send me back, so be it."

And right now some of you are thinking, "That sounds like fatalism; whatever happens, happens." It's not that at all; it's actually putting all your hope in God. It's praying for God to give you a vision for your life or family or marriage or career or education, and you go after it with all of your might. And you say, "God, this is what I'm going for, but the bottom line is, you do whatever you need to do. Not my will, but your will be done."

So, you have an option. You have the option of letting your emotions sweep you into self-destructive behaviors. Or you have the option of saying, just like the people who are reading this who've lost their spouse, but didn't lose hope; just like the people who are reading this who've lost children, but didn't lose hope; just like the people who are reading this who've lost all kinds of things, but didn't lose hope, you have the option of saying, "God, this really stinks and this is the opposite of what I had planned for and dreamed of, but God, do to me whatever you need to do. And whatever you do, I'm not going to turn my back on you because I know where that ends up. I accept it as coming from the hand of a loving Father." It's not fatalism; it's faith in a sovereign God. It's being able to see that whatever comes into our life, ultimately comes from the sovereign hand of God. And although I may never understand it, and it's not the way I would have designed it, I accept it as coming from the hand of a loving Heavenly Father.

The reality of life is that sometimes our dreams die; you've experienced that reality and so have I. Sometimes it's a part of God's grand scheme of things, but like with David and like with me also, sometimes it's the consequences of our own doing.

But when that happens, like in the story of the prodigal son, eventually we will return to God. And when we return, we're going to return with our hands in the air saying, "I don't like where the journey took me and I'm responsible for the outcome; I surrender." And we will come back with scars that we will have for the rest of our lives. And we will come back with memories that we won't be able to erase. And we will come back with some broken dreams and some busted up relationships that can't ever be repaired, but when we come back, our Heavenly Father will receive us back, because that's the kind of God He is; He's a God of grace and mercy. But I've got to be honest, He's not the kind of God that erases consequences. He loves us too much for that.

I have learned on my journey that it's in these times that we hold onto the truth of what God said in Jeremiah 29:11: "'For I know the plans I have for you,' declares the Lord, 'plans to prosper you and not to harm you, plans to give you hope and a future.'" Wouldn't you like to be there? That's what this book is all about. Regardless of our past, there is always a future with God, and therein lies our hope. But how do we get to that place? How do we help those who have fallen get to that place? Buckle in; you're in for a bumpy ride.

Chapter 2

"I've Got More Baggage Than Samsonite!"

There are a lot of things that you have to deal with when you are somewhat of a public figure and you blow it big time. One of the challenges is that you are recognized pretty much everywhere you go. I have run into people that attended the church where I pastored on islands in Hawaii, on cruise ships in the middle of the ocean, and at various airports around the world. In fact, it was rare to board an airplane without seeing someone that attended the church. So, you can imagine how I felt after my sin became public knowledge. I quickly realized that there was nowhere to hide. And at times, the shame of the whole situation became almost unbearable. There were days that I had dark thoughts that I never even thought were possible for me to have. I wouldn't wish it on anyone. I could deal with the guilt, but I hated the shame. Maybe you find yourself in a similar situation.

When it comes to shame, no one ever thinks of Jesus. In fact, If I were to ask you to make a list of twenty people that you felt were deserving of shame, you would probably list people like Adolph Hitler, Vladimir Putin, Jeffrey Dahmer, or Richard Ramirez, but I highly doubt that Jesus would make your list. And Jesus wouldn't make the list because we all know that He's not deserving of making the list. But did you know that Jesus also had to deal with shame? The writer of Hebrews 12:2 says: "…fixing our eyes on Jesus, the pioneer and perfecter of faith. For the joy set before Him he endured the cross, scorning its shame…"

That verse tells us that when Jesus was hanging on the cross, He despised the shame of it all. But even though He despised the shame, He followed through and died for the sins of the world.

Shame isn't new to the human race. It actually can be traced all the way back to the Garden of Eden. After Adam and Eve disobeyed God and ate the fruit from the Tree of the Knowledge and Good and Evil, it says in Genesis 3:7-8: "Then the eyes of both of them were opened, and they realized that they were naked; so they sewed fig leaves together and made coverings for themselves. Then the man and his wife heard the sound of the Lord God as he was walking in the garden in the cool of the day, and they hid from the Lord God among the trees of the garden."

Now understand, up until this point, Adam and Eve had never felt nor experienced shame before, but now they're naked and ashamed and they're trying to cover up. They try to hide from God and they try to hide from each other. And why did they hide? They were naked and ashamed and they have never experienced those emotions before. Genesis 3:9-11: "But the Lord God called to the man, 'Where are you?' He answered, 'I heard you in the garden, and I was afraid because I was naked; so I hid.' And he said, 'Who told you that you were naked?'"

Well, no one told them. It was that sense of shame because they knew they had done wrong.

By the way, who were they hiding from? It was just Adam and Eve and the animals. I don't care if the dog sees me naked. Now, cats, that's a different story! Don't ever trust a cat. So, who were they hiding from? They were hiding from God and they were hiding from each other. For the first time ever, they were ashamed of being naked. And so they made clothes to cover their shame. But look at what God does in Genesis 3:21: "The Lord God made garments of skin for Adam and his wife and clothed them." And for that to happen, something had to die. And that's the first hint in the Bible that the only thing that can cover our sin and shame is blood. It was like a preview of a coming attraction of the day when Jesus was going to shed His blood on the cross to cover our sin and shame. Let me show you a great verse in Isaiah 61:10: "I delight greatly in the Lord; my soul rejoices in my God. For he has clothed me with garments of salvation and arrayed me in a robe of his righteousness."

By the way, to be "righteous" means to be in a "right standing" with God. And the only way to be in a "right standing" with God is through what Jesus did for us on the cross. And when we accept what Jesus did for us, His righteousness is deposited into our account and our sin and shame is removed.

But here's the problem: Every one of us has blown it in some way since we began to follow Jesus. And why do I point out the fact that we all continue to screw up? It's because Satan loves to tell us, "You should be ashamed; there's nobody as bad as you are." And here's the right response to Satan's accusation, "You're exactly right, I'm not a good person and I've blown it, but God…" You see, that's called "being human." But God still loves you and He's forgiven you of all of your sin by putting the righteousness of his Son into your account. And when we realize this truth, while we often can get past the guilt of our sin, there is something about the embarrassing pain of shame that is beyond words. I know; I have lived there.

There seems to be an agony all its own connected with shame, and if you haven't been there recently, lucky you, but maybe you've forgotten the feeling that comes with it. Shame is far worse than guilt. Guilt is more a private thing. You keep it to yourself. You swallow it just as you sometimes swallow your pride, and you go on. But with shame, you can't just go on. There is that voice of the accuser constantly saying, "You, you, you…"

There is the story of a woman in John 8 that is one of the most intense scenes in the New Testament. I am confident that she had no idea that the sin she was involved in would be made public. I am sure she assumed that it would all take place in the privacy of her home under the cloak of darkness. But out of the blue she comes face to face with the Son of God who looked her in the eyes and dealt with her sin along with its disgrace and shame.

It all began early in the morning. The city of Jerusalem was probably still damp with dew. Long, purple shadows fell among the temple columns. Song birds chirped in the trees throughout the area. And in the midst of the tranquility of that morning, a small group of people had gathered for what we would call a small group or a Bible study. They had come to hear the words of Jesus, but little did they know what they were in for.

The story begins in John 8:1-2: "Jesus went to the Mount of Olives. At dawn He appeared again in the temple courts, where all the people gathered around Him, and he sat down to teach them." Then suddenly, Jesus is interrupted by a handful of men who came with stern faces and voices of hate. In John 8:3 they are referred to as the "self-righteous men of the city." They were the scribes and the Pharisees. These men couldn't stand Jesus and they hated His message of grace even more. In fact, they had one goal on their agenda and that was to put Him to death; they even had a plan. In fact, this whole scene was designed in order to trap Him.

But there was also someone who didn't belong in their midst; it wasn't a man; it was a woman. And she wasn't self-righteous; she was ashamed. The woman is never named here or anywhere else. Let me help you form a picture of her in your mind. Her hair was probably disheveled; her make-up was smeared; her nightgown may have been torn. Perhaps her arm is bruised and bleeding from the struggle she had had with these angry men. And as she is standing in front of this Bible study she must have thought, "How can they do this to me?"

After these men interrupt Jesus and His teaching, He stands to his feet and listens to their accusations in John 8:3-6: "The teachers of the law and the Pharisees brought in a woman caught in adultery. They made her stand before the group and said to Jesus, 'Teacher, this woman was caught in the act of adultery. In the Law, Moses commanded us to stone such women. Now what do you say?' They were using this question as a trap, in order to have a basis for accusing Him."

And so they bring this adulteress before Jesus and ask Him, "What do you think we should do with her?" In the Mishnah, the Jewish handbook, it stated that if a man was caught in adultery, he was to be strangled while standing knee deep in animal dung. If a woman was caught in adultery, she was to be stoned publicly.

Now, was she guilty of committing adultery? Of course she was guilty; she was caught in the very act. But Jesus, standing silently and observing the whole scene, didn't miss a clue. First, I'm sure Jesus thought, "How could this have taken place without it being a trap? You don't just stumble across a couple in the act of committing adultery. In fact, every effort is made to make sure that you don't get caught. The curtains are closed and the doors are locked. It must have been a trap." And I think Jesus' next thought was, "And where is the man?" Let me remind you of the phrase in John 8:6: "They were using this question as a trap, in order to have a basis for accusing Him." Jesus knew that. His class didn't know it; the woman didn't know it, but He knew it because He knew them. How was it a trap? First, if He said to stone her, they could call Him a hypocrite because Jesus was building his following on a message of compassion and forgiveness, and love and grace. And how could He be all of those things and say, "Kill her!" Furthermore, they could have turned Him over to the Roman government because the Jew lived under Roman rule and the Romans were the only ones who could declare capital punishment. That's why Jesus had to be taken before Pilate before He was crucified. Jesus had no authority to have this woman put to death. Jesus' second option was to encourage them to just let her go. But if He said to release her they could accuse Him of breaking the law of Moses. They could say that He condones adultery. They could label Him a law breaker.

By the way, where was the man? There are three possibilities. First possibility: he escaped, but that's doubtful because they certainly outnumbered this one man. If they could catch the woman, why not the man? Second possibility: the man could have deliberately been allowed to go free. That doesn't make sense because according to Jewish law, he was just as guilty as the woman. Third possibility: he was part of the group of men who were making the accusations. In other words, it was a set up and he helped set this woman up. So, these men are thinking that they finally have Jesus in a situation that He can't escape. He's between the proverbial "rock and a hard place." He's trapped.

But notice John 8:6: "Jesus bent down and started to write on the ground with his finger." By the way, this is the only time in the Bible where we are told that Jesus wrote anything. And what's interesting is the term that John uses when recording this. He uses the Greek word, *katagrapho*. Grapho is the root of the word; we get our English word, "graphic," from this Greek word. Kata means "down or against." The same word is used in Job 13:26: "For you write down bitter things against me." So, Jesus wrote something down in the sand. What did He write down? I think that, without saying a word, Jesus simply knelt down and began to write, large enough for the men to read, the secret sins that were hidden in their hearts. Maybe He wrote, "Idolater, liar, drunkard, murderer, adulterer." The silence is broken when Jesus stands up and looks into their self-righteous faces and says in John 8:7: "Let any one of you who is without sin be the first to throw a stone at her." In other words, "Go ahead, stone her; take your best shot. Just make sure that your hearts are pure and spotless and sinless. If that's the case, go for it."

After Jesus uttered those words, there must have been an aching silence; not a word was spoken; you could have heard a

pin drop. He looked at them and they stared at Him. John 8:8-9
says: "Again he stooped down and wrote on the ground. At this,
those who heard began to go away one at a time." And I'm sure
they stood there for a moment thinking about their lives, letting
it all pass in review, and they began to release their stones. The
only sound heard was the thud of stone after stone landing in
the sand. And one by one, these self-righteous men creep away
like animals slinking in the shadows. Can you imagine the hu-
miliation as they walked away just like you would and just like
I would?

The scene that follows is a study in contrast. Jesus is left alone
with this woman who deserved death but had been preserved
from it by the only one who was qualified to stone her. I would
have loved to have been in that Bible class. I would have loved
to have seen her face.

Nathaniel Hawthorne wrote in The Scarlet Letter: "The Scarlet Letter was her passport into regions where other women
dared not tread. Shame, despair, solitude — these had been her
teachers, stern and wild ones."

That's this woman. Having been caught in the act of adultery,
she stood before Jesus deserving death, and their eyes locked. I
doubt you could invent a more contrasting portrait to paint. A
woman; a man. A sinner; the sinless Son of God. An adulteress;
the Messiah. John 8:10 says: "Jesus straightened up and asked
her, 'Woman, where are they? Has no one condemned you?' The
only recorded words of this woman found in all of scripture are
located in John 8:11 when she answers, "No one sir." Isn't that a
great moment? And I think she even included herself. For the
first time in her life she understood what it meant to be free from
the awful guilt and shame of her life. "No one sir; not one."

And Jesus has this marvelous response John 8:11: "'Then neither do I condemn you,' Jesus declared. 'Go now and leave your
life of sin.'" This has been my experience: when legalism and
prejudice condemn, hate presides as the judge. When honesty

and compassion confront, love presides.

Isn't it remarkable that the only one who was qualified to condemn the woman, didn't? And I think for the first time in her life, she stopped condemning herself. I love what Paul wrote in Romans 8:1: "Therefore, there is now no condemnation for those who are in Christ Jesus." That was Jesus' message to this woman, and that is what the woman believes. And she is able to go and change her entire lifestyle because she refuses to be weighed down by shame.

I wish I had a magic wand that I could wave over everyone who is reading this and say, "Shame, be gone; self-condemnation, be gone." I wish I could wave it over my own life, but I can't. Just like you, I am limited to these written words and the work of the Spirit of God to take the words and drive them home. Some of you need to hear those words, "Shame, be gone; get out of my life. Condemnation, be gone; get out of my life." I need to be reminded of those words daily.

Two thoughts linger as I ponder this scene and I think about the topic of shame.

1st: All who are not qualified to condemn you, will; count on it. Those with hearts heavier than the stones in their hands will still throw the stones. My suggestion is, stay away from people like that; get far away from them.

2nd: The one who is qualified to condemn you, won't; stay close to Him.

We don't sing many hymns anymore, but in wrapping up this chapter, I want to share the story of a guy who wrote one of my favorite hymns; it has to deal with shame. William Cowper was from England. He lived a very immoral life before he became a Christian. Years later he got the opportunity to serve in the House of Lords and at first he was excited, but then he began to worry about his sordid past. He knew that there would be a public examination and eventually it would come out. He became so distraught over the shame of his past and the certainty of it being revealed that he tried to kill himself, not once, but four times, and each time failed. He tried to jump off of a bridge, but he was so afraid of heights, when he got to the apex of the bridge to jump, he chickened out. Then he went to a pharmacy and purchased a bottle of poison, but on the way home, he dropped the bottle and the bottle broke. He next tried to hang himself, but the beam he attached the rope to snapped. He then tried to stab himself, but the knife blade snapped. He was finally so exhausted from all of his failed suicide attempts that he fell asleep. The next morning when he woke up, there were some words going through his mind. He took a moment to write down the words, and through these words, God delivered him from his shame. And he went to the public examination and said, "I want to tell you about my past," and he told them about all of the sin and how Jesus had forgiven him. And there were people in the House of Lords that accepted Jesus as their Savior that day. These are the words he wrote:

There is a fountain filled with blood, drawn from Immanuel's veins,

And sinners plunged beneath that flood, lose all their guilty stains:

Lose all their guilty stains, lose all their guilty stains;

And sinners plunged beneath that flood, lose all their guilty stains.

Romans 8:1: "Therefore, there is now no condemnation for those who are in Christ Jesus."

Chapter 3

"Maybe There is Hope (but I'm Still Not Sure)!"

To say that the local church has played a big role in my life would be one of the great understatements of all time. I love the local church and I have always believed that the church is the hope of the world. And as Christians that make up the local church, our job is pretty clear; we've been called to follow in the footsteps of Jesus and to do the work of Jesus.

The problem is that we forget that during Jesus' earthly ministry, He did more than just show up at church or attend a small group occasionally. He spent the majority of His time reaching out and ministering to the hurting and broken and downcast and messed up people that were scattered across Palestine and Judea. If you don't believe that, you have my permission to put down this book and pick up your Bible and read the New Testament. In Matthew 11, Jesus exalted the lowly. In Mark 5, He released the captive. In Luke 4, He comforted the imprisoned. In Luke 15, He hung out with outsiders. In Luke 23, He forgave the criminal. In Luke 24, He consoled those who were mourning. In John 2, He gave water to the thirsty. In John 6, He fed the hungry. In John 21, He restored the fallen. Romans 4 says that He suffered for the sake of His people and Romans 5 says that He died in our place.

My point is, the Bible makes it very clear that Jesus was actively involved in ministering to people in need through love and grace and mercy, but that was only the beginning. Jesus told the Twelve in John 14:12: "Very truly I tell you, whoever believes in me will do the works I have been doing, and they will do even greater things than these, because I am going to the Father." In fact, He commanded the church to follow His example. That means that we can't just teach love and grace and mercy at church and then talk about those topics occasionally in our small groups. We have to also demonstrate love. We have to also demonstrate mercy. We have to also demonstrate grace.

And that's why the members of those early New Testament churches exhibited the same love and mercy and grace that Jesus exhibited. In Acts 6, they decided to take care of the widows in their community. In Acts 9, they forgave the criminal. In Acts 11, they fed the hungry and they fellowshipped with outsiders. In Acts 16, they comforted the imprisoned and released the captive. In Acts 20, they consoled the mourning. In 1 Corinthians 1, they exalted the lowly. In 2 Corinthians 2, they restored the fallen. Colossians 1 tells us that they suffered for the sake of God's people.

So, it's pretty clear that the church, from its conception, was actively involved in ministering to a hurting, broken world. And we who follow Jesus are charged with continuing to carry out that work, and that requires us to address, with our actions, the hurts and needs and brokenness that confront us and surround us daily. We, not the government, are commanded to visit the sick and imprisoned. We, not the government, are commanded to seek out and find lost sheep. We, not the government, are commanded to bring healing to a broken world. We, not the government, are commanded to restore broken lives. We, not the government, are commanded to lift up the downtrodden. We, not the government, are commanded to be the hands and feet and mouthpiece of Jesus Christ to our world.

This is what Jesus said in Mark 2:17: "It is not the healthy who need a doctor, but the sick. I have not come to call the righteous, but sinners." The church has often been compared to a hospital where the hurting, broken and downcast can come to be healed. Here's my question: If that analogy is accurate, why aren't the hurting, broken and downcast people showing up? The fact is, church involvement and attendance in our country are at an all-time low, and it can't be because there's no broken-ness, pain and heartache around us; we all know that's not the case. There has never been more despair and hopelessness in our world than we are witnessing today, but fewer and fewer people are walking into the doors of our churches looking for hope, healing and restoration than ever. As a result, the church is becoming increasingly irrelevant in our culture. Do you know why? It's because most churches do a good job of teaching love, mercy and grace, but many churches often fail miserably at showing and extending love, mercy and grace to the bruised, brokenhearted and downcast outside the church, and even more so, to those already inside the church.

And so in this chapter, I want to talk about how to love unlovable, difficult, messy, broken, sinful people. By the way, does anyone in your life fit that description? If you can't think of anyone, I'll help you identify them. When you see this person's number show up on your cell phone, you don't answer it. If this person is going to be attending a family event, you make the choice not to attend. Instead of wanting to be involved in restoring this person, you find much more joy and satisfaction in judging and punishing this individual. You often have the attitude, "They deserve whatever consequences that come their way because they brought it on themselves." And maybe you even hate the way you feel about that individual. You feel guilty about it, but no matter how hard you try, you can't change it. Now that I've helped, do you have at least one person in your life that fits this description? How many of you are that person? I am.

But I really believe that one of the characteristics of a Christ follower is that we can learn to love people that we would never naturally love on our own. In fact, just think how Jesus modeled that attitude while he was on this earth. He hung out with tax collectors and prostitutes and adulteresses. Even with His dying breath, Jesus invited a thief to spend eternity with Him. And after Jesus ascended back to Heaven, His followers took his example very seriously. In fact, notice what Paul wrote to a small church in Colossians 3:11: "Here there is no Gentile or Jew, circumcised or uncircumcised, barbarian, Scythian, slave or free, but Christ is all, and is in all." What's that all about? These are references to people who had hated one another for centuries, but now they find themselves sitting beside each other in this little church in the city of Colossae.

And Paul explains why this kind of fellowship and love and unity is possible. First of all, it's because there's no more hostility between the Jews and Greeks. Why is that significant? It's because, in the minds of the first-century Jew, if you weren't Jewish you were unclean; you were a pagan. And so, a Jew wouldn't eat with you or speak to you or touch you if you weren't a Jew. But now the Jews and Greeks are singing and worshiping and serving together in this small church.

Paul also refers to those who were slaves and those who were free. And that means nothing until you understand that in the first-century slaves weren't even thought of as human beings. In fact, Aristotle referred to slaves as "living tools with no rights." Slaves had no right to be married or to have a family. They could be beaten, even killed by their owners and nothing would be done about it. Historians believe that a third of the population of Colossae may have been slaves, but now we have slaves and free sitting next to each other in this church

Then there were the Barbarians. I just mentioned how much the Jews hated the Greeks? The Greeks had just as much contempt for the Barbarians. In fact, the word "barbarian" comes from the Greeks. When they heard someone speaking any language other than Greek, they'd go, "bar, bar, bar." Obviously the first-century Greeks weren't very mature, but that's where the term "barbarian" came from.

But the Scythians were a particularly interesting group of

Barbarians. They were thought of as the lowest of the low, the most barbaric. In fact, they were often referred to in extra-biblical literature as "wild beasts." To "behave like a Scythian" was a metaphor in the first century for bad behavior. If you drank too much and you lived a wild and crazy lifestyle, you were called a Scythian. In our day, we call them "those people." By the way, who are the "those people" in your life, and be honest? Is it the Democrats, or the Republicans, or the rich, or the poor, or the Black, or the White, or the Hispanic, or the Muslims, or the LGBT community? Who do you see as "the enemy?" In Colossae, the Scythians and the Barbarians are sitting down next to the cultured and the sophisticated. The uneducated are sitting next to the educated. The powerful are sitting next to the powerless. The wealthy are sitting next to the poor.

Now, that doesn't mean that there were no conflicts. In Acts 6, we're told about a conflict between the Greek-speaking Christians and the Hebrew-speaking Christians. In Galatians 1, there was a conflict between circumcised Christians and uncircumcised Christians. The book of Philemon was written because of a conflict between a Christian slave and a Christian slave-owner. In Romans, there's an intense conflict between those Christians who were strong in their faith and those who were weak in their faith. Paul wrote to the church at Corinth, "There are quarrels and divisions among you." You can read about difficult, broken people throughout the New Testament. In other words, just because someone is a Christian doesn't automatically mean that they are easy to love. You may even consider that individual an enemy. But I believe that Paul is teaching us that the real test of spiritual maturity is the ability to love unlovable people, but that's easier said than done, isn't it? And maybe that's why the church has such a horrible track record in this area.

There's an old hymn we used to sing at the Baptist church I grew up in. It was entitled, "Onward Christian Soldiers." The first line went, "Onward Christian Soldiers, marching as to war…" If that analogy is accurate, and it is, then I would say that the church is the only army that has a track record for shooting its wounded instead of nursing them back to health. And maybe that's the reason that there are so many hurting people staying away from church these days. Maybe it's because they have watched and observed and listened to how we actually treat the bruised and broken hearted within our own ranks and they've come to the conclusion, "Thanks, but no thanks. I'll take my chances out here among the wolves."

What makes this even more sad is that addressing the needs of the hurting and bruised and brokenhearted and the messy and unlovable is the very reason Jesus came. In fact, this is how Jesus described his own ministry in Luke 4:18: "The Spirit of the Lord is on me, because he has anointed me to proclaim good news to the poor. He has sent me to proclaim freedom for the prisoner and recovery of sight for the blind to set the oppressed free." That was the plan from day one. That was His target audience. Let me explain why I say that.

If you've been around church for a while, you know that there are four different accounts of the life of Jesus in the Bible. These four accounts are found in the New Testament books known as Matthew, Mark, Luke, and John. These guys are not to be confused with the band members that made up the Beatles. They were followers of Jesus and they eventually wrote the four books that we now know as the gospels. These four books record the life and times of Jesus. And what's interesting is that two of these four accounts don't say anything about the birth of Jesus. Mark and John both begin with the ministry of John the Baptist just before Jesus goes public with His ministry around the age of thirty. But Matthew and Luke both begin with the birth of Jesus. Luke begins with Gabriel announcing to Zechariah and Elizabeth that they're going to have a baby; that baby will be John the Baptist. And then Gabriel appears to Mary and tells her that she's going to give birth to the Son of God, Jesus. But

Matthew begins his book with the genealogy of Jesus.

Matthew 1:1-2 says, "This is the genealogy of Jesus the Messiah the son of David, the son of Abraham: Abraham was the father of Isaac, Isaac the father of Jacob, Jacob the father of Judah and his brothers…" and Matthew goes on and on right up to the birth of Jesus. And to be honest, it's not all that interesting. In fact, most of us don't even waste our time reading it; we skip right over it. And since that's the case, you may wonder why Matthew even bothered to write it. Well, Matthew, who was a Jew, is writing to Jews and he's about to make the case that Jesus is the Messiah, the Son of God. And he knew that the first question a Jewish audience was going to ask before they read any further was, "Is Jesus related to David because if Jesus isn't related to David, we can't take Him seriously because God promised that David would have a descendant on the throne." So, knowing that, Matthew decides, "Let's begin by addressing the elephant in the room right up front," and so he begins with Jesus' genealogy.

Now, let me point out something that you may find interesting, but it also comes into play in the Book of Matthew. In ancient times, the only recorded history was written by hired historians, and whoever hired the historian made sure that history was written in a way that made them look good. The goal was to make sure that the good stuff was highlighted, and the negative stuff was left out. But when you read this ancient document that Matthew wrote, Matthew goes out of his way to make us question some of the people in Jesus' family tree. In fact, he mentions people that he didn't need to mention at all.

First of all, this should have been a male-only list because Matthew is trying to connect Jesus the man to David the man. But Matthew goes out of his way to give us the names of four women, and as you're going to see, he should have probably left out two of these women. And to make it even more confusing, three of the four women aren't even Jewish. And so Matthew goes out of his way to say, "Oh yea, this Messiah that I'm going to talk about doesn't even have a pure Jewish bloodline." I can assure you, that didn't help his argument with this Jewish audience. For example, in Matthew 1:3, Matthew talks about Judah the father of Perez and Zerah, whose mother was Tamar (a different Tamar than King David's daughter mentioned earlier). Now, we'll look at this Tamar later on, but I'll tell you ahead of time, her story is salacious and scandalous. In fact, there are some parts of the story about Tamar that I couldn't even read in church. And having mentioned that, right now, some of you men are tempted to put down this book and pick up your Bible and locate the story of Tamar. But when we get to her story later on, you're going to see that Matthew would have had a much stronger case about Jesus being the Messiah by just leaving out Tamar, yet Matthew pauses and throws in Tamar.

The genealogy continues in Matthew 1:4-5, "Ram the father of Amminadab, Amminadab the father of Nahshon, Nahshon the father of Salmon, Salmon the father of Boaz, whose mother was Rahab..." Rahab isn't Jewish either. And if you've been around church for a while, you know that Rahab had a nickname, didn't she? She wasn't just Rahab; she was Rahab the harlot. I mean, when we get to Heaven and meet Rahab, we're going to go, "Oh yea! You're Rahab the...lady in the Old Testament." There was no reason to bring up Rahab in Jesus' genealogy. But since Matthew included her, I've concluded that Rahab the harlot, not Santa, put the "Ho! Ho! Ho!" in Christmas. Matthew 1:5 continues, "Boaz the father of Obed, whose mother was Ruth..." And the story of Ruth is a great story, but Ruth wasn't Jewish. Ruth was from Moab and every Jew knew that.

And it really gets crazy in Matthew 1:5-6: "Obed the father of Jesse, and Jesse the father of King David. David was the father of Solomon, whose mother had been Uriah's wife." And Matthew doesn't even have to mention the woman's name, but everybody knew that it was Bathsheba. And you don't even have to be a church person to know about David and Bathsheba. You know that David committed adultery with Bathsheba and then had her husband, Uriah, killed to try and cover up the whole thing. And I'm sure these Jewish readers were thinking, "Why did you have to go there? Why couldn't you just focus on the great things about David?" My point is, it's almost as if Matthew is going out of his way to twist the knife. Why all of the distractions? Why not just stick with the men's names? And if he's going to mention women, why doesn't he mention Sarah, or Rebecca, or Deborah? They are all Jewish women with incredible stories. But, instead, he mentions Tamar and Rahab and Solomon's mother who WAS (emphasis on "past tense") Uriah's wife."

Let me answer that question. It's because Matthew spent three years with Jesus. Matthew heard Jesus teach. Matthew saw Jesus heal the sick and raise the dead. Matthew saw Jesus die on a cross. Matthew stood next to an empty tomb. And Matthew knew that all of these shady characters in the genealogy of Jesus with all of their baggage, sin and embarrassing stories were the main point of the story he was about to tell. Matthew knew that sin was the issue that Jesus came to address. He knew that Jesus didn't just come FOR sinners. Matthew wanted the world to know that Jesus came FROM sinners, and that was okay, because that was the point. Matthew knew firsthand that this really was a story about light coming into darkness. This really was a story of forgiveness coming into a world that only knew condemnation. This really was a story about grace coming into a world that had only experienced the harshness and the rules and regulations of the Law. But Matthew also knew that this was HIS story, and that the people like Rahab, Judah, Tamar and Bathsheba were his kinds of people. Just like Matthew, they were lost and without hope, but everything changed for Matthew on the day he met Jesus.

Matthew's story began in the little town of Capernaum on

the coast of the Sea of Galilee. Let's pick up the story in Matthew 9:1-5: "Jesus stepped into a boat, crossed over and came to his own town. Some men brought to Him a paralyzed man, lying on a mat. When Jesus saw their faith, he said to the man, 'Take heart, son; your sins are forgiven'. At this, some of the teachers of the law said to themselves, 'This fellow is blaspheming!' [These Jews knew that only God can forgive sins and so Jesus is claiming to be God] Knowing their thoughts, Jesus said, 'Why do you entertain evil thoughts in your hearts? Which is easier: to say, "Your sins are forgiven," or to say, "Get up and walk"?'"

And we don't know if Matthew was present at this event or if he heard about it after the fact, but we do know about those moments later on when Matthew was eyeball-to-eyeball with Jesus for the very first time. Let's pick up the story in Matthew 9:9: "As Jesus went on from there, he saw a man named Matthew sitting at the tax collector's booth."

Now, let me put this scene into context. I recently had a conversation with someone at dinner and I was asked, "What was your most embarrassing moment in life?" Well, it was when I was informed that a video announcement was sent out by email to thousands of people to inform them that I had been involved in an "adulterous affair." Obviously it had to be addressed in some fashion; that wasn't what made it so embarrassing; I knew that it was coming. But because I didn't know that the announcement had already gone out, I obviously wasn't prepared for people's reaction to the video. And so, I'm in a restaurant and a guy I didn't know walked up to me and informed me that he had just watched the announcement. He could tell that I was shocked and obviously caught off guard. Once he realized that I wasn't aware of what had happened, he pulled out his phone and showed it to me. He could not have been more gracious and merciful. He even gave me a hug and informed me that he would be praying for me. But it was one of those moments that we all have in life. You remember right where you were and exactly what you were doing. I wanted to crawl into a hole and never come out.

In the same way, this had to have been Matthew's most embarrassing moment. I'm sure he was looking for the nearest hole and I'll tell you why. During the time of Jesus, the Jews lived under Roman rule and the Jews hated it. And one of the things they really hated were the relentless taxes posed on them by Rome. There were income taxes and bridge taxes and gate taxes. There were taxes on meat and fruit and camels, in fact, everything was taxed. And so, as you can imagine, the problem for the Romans was actually collecting these taxes from the Jews, and the reason it was such a problem was because it was so dangerous. If you were a Roman trying to collect taxes from Jews who were living in an occupied territory, you were taking your life into your own hands. I'm guessing that your house got egged and the tires on your chariot were slashed on a regular basis. Your kids were probably bullied at school and on social media.

And so the Romans came up with the brilliant idea of recruiting Jewish citizens to collect the taxes from their own Jewish people. In fact, if you were a Jew and you had the money, you could buy a tax-collecting franchise! And this was a very lucrative endeavor because tax collectors could overtax the people and keep the profits. In other words, as long as Rome got their portion, they didn't care what you charged. But as you can imagine, from the Jew's perspective, this was about the worst job a Jew could have. You were betraying your nation and you were betraying God. As a result, you were considered a traitor; you were an outcast. In fact, tax collectors had a lower approval rating than congress. And that's why, when you read the New Testament, you always see tax collectors and sinners grouped together. It's because tax collectors were considered to be the lowest of the low.

Well, Matthew was a tax collector. And I'm sure he was an

embarrassment to his family. His own people ostracized him. I'm sure he wasn't allowed in the synagogue or the temple. My guess is that his only friends were other tax collectors and sinners. And so Matthew, who is a Jew, is sitting at his tax collector's booth collecting taxes from other Jews when Jesus walks up, and Jesus is followed by His disciples who also hate tax collectors. And you know that Peter, Andrew and John are already thinking about what they're going to say as they pass by Matthew. Maybe they will even spit at him and give him the old stink eye. But Jesus says to Matthew in Matthew 9:9, "Follow me…why don't you come with us?" Can you picture this scene? I'm sure that, other than the crucifixion, this had to be the worst day in Peter's life. I'm sure he was thinking, "Jesus, you're kidding right? You want him to come with us?"

By the way, preachers like to make a big deal over the fact that Matthew left his tax collector's booth and followed Jesus and never looked back, but we don't know that; that's not in the story. In fact, I doubt that actually happened. He had a job. He had a responsibility. He had bills to pay. But on this day, he apparently turned over the responsibilities to his assistant, and he got up and followed Jesus. And I'm sure that Matthew asked, "Just curious, where are we going?" And Jesus responded, "How about your house?" And Peter had to be thinking, "Hell will freeze over and I will ice skate on it before I go into a tax collector's house! Everybody already thinks we're weirdos. Just being seen talking to him is embarrassing enough." But Jesus was like, "Let's go to your house, and why don't you invite some of your friends too; we'll order pizza." And who does Matthew invite? He invites more tax collectors and sinners, after all, they're the only people that would hang out with him.

And all the religious people who had been keeping an eye on Jesus gathered outside of Matthew's home. They can't go inside because they would then be considered unclean because tax collectors had cooties, I guess. And Matthew 9:11 says, "When the Pharisees saw this, they asked his disciples, 'Why does your teacher eat with tax collectors and sinners?'" In other words, "We don't understand your teacher. On one hand He talks about the righteousness of God and He seems to want to uphold the Law. But now He's inside this tax collector's house getting tax collector cooties! We don't understand." And either Jesus overhears the conversation or His disciples let Him know what's being discussed. And so Jesus walks outside and He says to these religious leaders in Matthew 9:12, "It is not the healthy who need a doctor, but the sick."

And let's be honest: At this point, Matthew and all of his sinning friends know that Jesus is referring to them as "the sick," and they could have easily been offended, but they weren't, because do you know what people know who are far from God? They know that they are far from God. Some of you know that about yourself right now. And if I were to judge you and say, "You're far from God," it would be offensive, and you would probably tell me where to put my religion. But deep down inside, you know. It's kind of like the story of the guy who owned a pet store and he had a large, talking parrot sitting at the entrance where the patrons entered. Well, there was a customer who shopped at the store on a regular basis and every time he entered the store the parrot would say to the customer, "You're ugly!" This took place every week for months. Eventually the customer informed the owner that he would never shop at the store again unless the owner could get his parrot under control. Not wanting to lose a long time customer, the owner told the parrot to never tell the customer that he was ugly again or he couldn't be at the entrance to the shop. A few days later the customer returned to the store. When he walked in, he looked at the parrot and the parrot looked at him. The parrot looked away and the man looked away. The parrot once again stared at the man and the man once again stared back at the parrot. After a long intense pause the parrot said, "You know!" In the same way,

Matthew knew. He may have even had the thought, "I never considered myself sick, but I get where Jesus is coming from. And when it comes to being a righteous person, yea, I'm sick."

And then Jesus said in Matthew 9:13: "But go and learn what this means: 'I desire mercy, not sacrifice.'" That's a quote from the story of Hosea in the Old Testament. And then Jesus concluded by saying, "'For I have not come to call the righteous, but sinners.'" And that didn't offend Matthew and his friends because they knew they were sinners. And I think that as Matthew sat down and thought about the story that he was about to write, and as he thought through his own story, he knew that to include sinners in the genealogy of Jesus wasn't the exception; it was the point; it was because he had seen Jesus live out the mission, "I didn't come to call the righteous, but the sinners. I didn't come for those who think they are healthy; I came for those who realize that they are sick." And I think that Matthew understood that better than any of the other gospel writers. He understood that the story is about God drawing near to those who had drawn away from Him. It's about God leaning into those who had leaned away from Him. And Matthew knew that he needed to highlight these shady characters in the genealogy of Jesus because those people reflected why Jesus came.

And at the end of three years with Jesus, Matthew had discovered that when Jesus came to this earth, He changed the rules about what it meant to approach God. Because up until Jesus, the approach to God was, "I approach God on the basis of what I have and haven't done. And the only reason that God will take me seriously is if I've done good things and if I've done my best to avoid bad things." And Matthew knew, "If that's the platform for approaching God, I've got no chance with God ever." But what Matthew discovered after watching Jesus for three years was that the rules had changed. And that he, who had failed in every way possible, had an opportunity to have a relationship with God, not on the basis of what he had done, but on the basis of what Jesus had done for him. Isn't that awesome? And I believe that Matthew must have smiled every time he got to one of those seedy characters as he wrote this genealogy.

I want to introduce you to some of these characters throughout this book. Maybe you've heard their stories before, maybe not. But their story is our story. And my goal is this: If you still approach God based on what you've done for God, I hope that you will abandon that approach completely. Because, no matter how good you are, or how consistently you've attended church, or how many times you've been to confession, or how much you give or serve others, it's not good enough. And so, my goal is that we'll abandon this approach to God. And if you are a person who's afraid to approach God because of what you've done, I want to change your perspective on that. Maybe there are things in your life that you're so ashamed of you can't even comprehend approaching God. Maybe there is just too much baggage, or immorality, or disobedience and chaos, so you've given up on ever having a relationship with God. I understand; I've been there recently, too. My hope is that this book will allow you to abandon that whole way of thinking, because your relationship with God isn't about what you've done or how bad you've been; it's all about what He did for you. This book is for those who think they are righteous, and it's for those who know they're not. And my goal is that all of us would come to the place where we can say with a clear conscience, "God, in my prayers, in my thinking, in my perspective, and in my world view, I'm not coming to you based on anything I have or haven't done. I'm coming to you 100% based on the fact that, through Jesus, you have done something for me. And when I pray to you or think about you, I'm not going to run it through the grid of what I have or haven't done because I believe that when you sent Jesus into this world, He didn't come to be a helper or a coach or to give me a second chance. I believe that you sent your Son, Jesus to be exactly what Matthew presented Him to be; He came to be my Savior."

Now, I'll warn you, it's more difficult than you may think to abandon the, "I can make it happen myself," approach to God. After my fall, I spent weeks away at a counseling center trying to wrap my head around this very truth because I was 100% confident that because of what I had done, God wanted absolutely nothing to do with me. And to be honest, I'm still not sure yet. And it's because my entire life I've believed that the quality of my relationship with God was based on what I did and didn't do. So, I promise you, the longer you've been around church and the better you think you are, the more difficult this is going to be. Self-righteousness will eat your lunch. You will believe the lie that you're okay and that everyone else is the problem. You will never truly understand your desperate need for love and grace and forgiveness, and acceptance and restoration. And that explains why it wasn't the tax gatherers, or the sinners, or even the Romans that crucified Jesus. It was the men and women that believed they somehow had an approach to God based on their goodness. It was the group who never understood, "I have not come to call the self-righteous; I have come to call sinners."

You can continue to see this throughout the genealogy of Jesus. For example, most of us are familiar with the story of Rahab the Harlot, but Rahab is in the genealogy of Jesus (and I'll say more about her at the end of the book). All of us, whether we grew up in church or not, are familiar with the story of David and Bathsheba. It's a story of adultery and murder and deceit. Yet David is listed among those in Jesus' family tree. But you're probably not as familiar with the story of Judah, and the story of Judah may be the most salacious story of them all.

Matthew writes in Matthew 1:1-2: "This is the genealogy of Jesus the Messiah, the son of David, the son of Abraham: Abraham was the father of Isaac, Isaac the father of Jacob, Jacob the father of Judah and his brothers..." Now, if I were to ask you to share with a friend everything you know about Judah, it would probably be a short conversation. But Judah had a very famous brother that you are familiar with. His name is Joseph. Maybe you saw the musical, but he was the kid who had the coat of many colors because he was his daddy's favorite. And so most people at least know something about Joseph, but very few people know much about Judah. But Joseph isn't mentioned in the genealogy of Jesus, instead it's Judah. And after you hear his story, this is the question you're going to be asking yourself, "Why did God choose Judah over Joseph to be in Jesus' family tree when everything about Joseph's story is remarkable?" He had great character, great discipline, and great faith. In fact, in the Book of Genesis, he's seen as a Savior. He saves his family. He saves Pharaoh. He even saves the nation of Egypt. If there was ever a perfect picture of Jesus in the Old Testament, it was Joseph. But God looked at the twelve brothers and said, "I think I'll pick Judah." But I'll tell you ahead of time, after you hear this story, you would never pick Judah. And so why does God pick him? It's because that's the point of the gospel.

The story unfolds in Genesis 37. By this time, Judah and his brothers are already very jealous of Joseph. And to make matters worse, Jacob, the father in the story, makes the beautiful coat for Joseph. And one day, all of Joseph's brothers are out in the field working, and Joseph walks up wearing his special coat. Let's pick up the story in Genesis 37:23-24: "So when Joseph came to his brothers, they stripped him of his robe—the ornate robe he was wearing— and they took him and threw him into the cistern. The cistern was empty; there was no water in it." Now get the picture: They've just thrown their brother into this cistern naked. Genesis 37:25: "As they sat down to eat their meal..." And Joseph is down in that pit and he's probably yelling, "Hey guys, are you still up there; this isn't funny anymore?" And the brothers are sitting around eating their KFC saying, "Do you guys hear something?" And as they're eating their lunch, they look up and spot these traders headed to Egypt. And Genesis 37:26 says, Judah (there's our guy) said to his brothers, "What will we gain if we kill our brother and cover up his blood?" And the brothers think, "That's true ! If we just kill him, we don't have anything to gain from that. Is there a way to leverage this for our benefit?" Now, let me introduce you to Judah, through whom our Savior came. Judah isn't the oldest of the brothers, but he was the influencer. And so Judah responds in Genesis 37:27, "'Come, let's sell him to the Ishmaelites and not lay our hands on him; after all, he is our brother, our own flesh and blood.' His brothers agreed." But mercy kicks in and the brothers conclude, "Let's not kill him; let's just sell him." And the brothers sell Joseph to the Ishmaelites and the Ishmaelites take Joseph off to be a slave in Egypt. And I'm sure Judah thought, "That's the last time we will ever see Joseph." And the brothers kill an animal and they take the fancy coat and smear it with animal blood, and they go home and break mom and dad's hearts by telling them that Joseph was killed by a wild animal. And these brothers make a bond to carry this secret to their graves. In fact, they carry that guilt for twenty years. And Judah never breaks; he never confesses, but he knows in his heart that he's ultimately responsible because he's the influencer. And there's nothing ever said about any of the other brothers, but there is one chapter in Genesis dedicated to a story about Judah, and in this story, Judah goes from bad to downright creepy.

After the whole Joseph deal, Judah moves on with his life and eventually he gets married and he has a bunch of kids. His first three kids are boys. And when his firstborn son, Er, is old enough, Judah marries him off to a woman named Tamar (I mentioned her earlier). But Genesis 38:7 says: "Er, Judah's first born, was wicked in the Lord's sight; so the Lord put him to death." Judah's second son was named Onan and Onan also gets married. And this is what Genesis 37:10 says about Onan: "What he did was wicked in the Lord's sight; so the Lord put him to death also." Judah also has a third son named Shelah, but Shelah was too young to marry. And so Judah goes to Tamar, his daughter-in-law, because, according to the traditions of the day, he's now responsible for her. And Judah tells Tamar, "Live as a single woman until Shelah is old enough and then I'll have him marry you, and he'll take care of you and protect you and provide for you." So, Tamar moves back in with her parents and she waits for Shelah to grow up so she can marry him. According to tradition, that was her only option.

Well, years goes by, and Judah forgets all about marrying Tamar off to his younger son, and Tamar finds herself in a position where she can't provide for herself. So, Tamar decides to take matters into her own hands in Genesis 38:13-16: "When Tamar was told, 'Your father-in-law is on his way to Timnah to shear his sheep, she took off her widow's clothes, covered herself with a veil to disguise herself (that was the sign of a temple prostitute), and then sat down at the entrance to Enaim, which is on the road to Timnah. For she saw that, though Shelah had now grown up, she had not been given to him as his wife. When Judah saw her, he thought she was a prostitute, for she had covered her face. Not realizing that she was his daughter-in-law, he went over to her by the roadside and said, 'Come now, let me sleep with you.'"

So, Judah hires her as a prostitute, and they decide that the payment for this transaction will be a goat. I guess that was the going rate 3,000 years ago. And after their time together, Judah tells her, "I'll send you a goat." And she responds, "As security, I want two things. I want your seal and it's cord, (which represented his reputation), and I want your staff (which represented strength)." Both were a really big deal at this time in Hebrew history. And since Judah doesn't have a goat with him, he doesn't have much of a choice, and so he agrees. And when Judah gets home, he finds a servant and says, "On my recent trip, I met a prostitute and I owe her a goat; don't ask any questions. I just need you to go and find her and give her a goat." And the servant takes off with the goat, but he can't find this prostitute anywhere. So, he goes back home and tells Judah that he can't find her. And over time, Judah decides to just forget the whole thing. But Geneses 38:24 says, "About three months later Judah was told, 'Your daughter-in-law Tamar is guilty of prostitution, and as a result she is now pregnant.'" And then Judah does what every person does who has a secret and who's pretending to be something they're not; Judah gets real, self-righteous, and he responds in Genesis 38:24: "'Bring her out and have her burned to death!'" And he gets the community all jacked up and they're going to burn Tamar alive at the stake.

But Tamar has something that belongs to Judah, doesn't she? And notice what Tamar did in Genesis 38:25: "As she was being brought out, she sent a message to her father-in-law. 'I am pregnant by the man who owns these,' she said. And she added, 'See if you recognize whose seal and cord and staff these are.'" And Judah is like, "Change of plans; no fire today; bad idea." And he goes to see Tamar and he says to her, "Tamar, you're more righteous than me because I didn't do what I said I would do." And as a result, Tamar is allowed to live and eventually she gives birth to a little boy and his name is Perez and he's in the genealogy of Jesus.

And we read this story about a man, a prostitute and a goat and think, "Dang, Matthew; I don't believe I'd told that!" I mean, this is the kind of thing that ends up on The Jerry Springer Show! You've got a kid born out of wedlock and his parents are a man and his daughter-in-law who was posing as a prostitute! I'm thinking, "Matthew, that's the kind of thing you keep quiet; that's the kind of scandal you hope nobody ever discovers," unless it's the point of the story.

But the story isn't over for Judah because about twenty years after he and his brothers sell Joseph into slavery, there's a famine in the land. So, Jacob, the father, calls his sons together and tells them that they have to go to Egypt to buy grain, and so they take off for Egypt. And guess who's in charge of the grain? It's Joseph who is now the Prime Minister of Egypt. Now, Joseph was a teenager the last time the brothers saw him, but now he's thirty-something years old. And Joseph dresses like an Egyptian, and he talks like an Egyptian, and he walks like an Egyptian, and so they didn't recognize him, but he recognizes them. And if you're familiar with the story you know that he plays some mind games with them, and he puts them through the wringer because he wants to know if they've changed. It's a great story and you really need to read it, but this is how it all culminates. Eventually, all of these brothers are in a room alone with Joseph, but they still don't know it's him. And he takes off his Egyptian headpiece, and he says, "I am Joseph, your brother!" At that moment, I'm sure it was quieter than a grave yard at midnight. And I'm also sure that Judah is thinking, "What would I do if the roles were reversed? What would I do to the brother who sold me into slavery?" And Judah knows what he would do and it's because Judah knows his own character. But now he's standing before the man who has the power over life and death.

And Joseph says, "I forgive you. In fact, I'm going to take care of you and your families." And then later on Joseph says in Genesis 50:20: "You intended to harm me, but God intended it for good to accomplish what is now being done, the saving of many lives." "I saved you. I saved your families. I saved Pharaoh and I saved the Egyptians." And in this story, Joseph is a picture of a savior, but when it came to the genealogy of Jesus, God said, "I think I'll skip the savior and go with the creepy one, and I'll bring my son into the world through Judah, not Joseph."

And Matthew underscores that little snippet of history in his genealogy, and it was because, on that day in front of Joseph, Judah was a picture of you and me, and that's the point of the gospel. Judah was the picture of a person who deserved one thing, but God did something else. He was the picture of someone who learned that God's grace and mercy and forgiveness is available. In fact, God's grace and mercy and forgiveness is available to people who haven't even made themselves available to God.

Think about it, Judah never broke, or confessed, or apologized. But at the apex of this story, Joseph gives Judah the opposite of what he deserved. And God decided to skip Joseph, the righteous one, and to choose Judah, the unrighteous one. And it was through Judah that He brought His Son into this world.

Doesn't that just blow your mind? But that's the point of the gospel. It's the story that no one has ever been expected to come to God on the basis of their own righteousness or goodness; that's never been the plan. And neither did God ever intend for anyone, regardless of their sin or their past to say, "I'll never be at peace with God because of what I've done, " or, "I'll never be at peace with God because of what I haven't done." "I'll never be at peace with God because I destroyed a relationship." Or, "I'll never be at peace with God because I committed adultery," or, "I'll never be at peace with God because I hurt someone, and I've never taken responsibility. And since I can't change the past, I can't do anything to fix my relationship with God." From the very beginning, that has never been the plan. That's mankind's made-up religious approach to God. But as far back as the Book of Genesis, God gives us a picture of grace and mercy and forgiveness because what God knows about the human soul is that self-righteousness has never made a person better. The fear of God has never made a person better. Promising to do better has never been able to do anything about our past. It does nothing about the relationships that we've destroyed. It does nothing about the brokenness that we've created in other people's lives. Our only hope has nothing to do with what we've done; it has everything to do with what's been done for us.

So, when Matthew starts out he says, "Before we even get to the Jesus part, I want to remind you of how it's always been. From the very beginning, God has chosen the broken and messed up people of this world, and these are people that have access to Him. But it wasn't because of what they did; it was based on what had been done, and in the New Testament, would be done, for them." And that's so wonderful because that's your story and that's my story. That's the story of the gospel. It's that God came into this world to extend grace to people who didn't deserve it.

And this is what I've finally learned after my failure and after all of my years of being a performance-based Christian. And it changes us. When we discover that what's most important in our lives is a relationship with God, not our past. When we discover that what's most important in our lives is finding peace with God, not trying to fix ourselves. When we discover that the key to approaching God has nothing to do with what we've done, it's about what God has done for us. When that truth explodes in our minds and shapes the view of how we see ourselves and how God sees us. All of that begins to change us on the inside. And that's when we find the grace to deal with our past, and that's when we find the grace to forgive ourselves. It never begins with, "This is what I've done and this is what I promise to do." It always begins with, "This is what has been done for me through Jesus Christ."

So, let me ask you a question: Are you a person who thinks that you can never have peace with God because of your past? If that describes you, then I have great news. God is drawing near to you even though you've allowed your past to draw you away from Him. His grace is available to you even if you've never made yourself available to Him, and we see that in the life of Judah.

But that' not the end because the genealogy continues in Matthew 1:3-5: "Judah the father of Perez and Zerah, whose mother was Tamar, Perez the father of Hezron, Hezron the father of Ram, Ram the father of Amminadab, Amminadab the father of Nahshon, Nahshon the father of Salmon, Salmon the father of Boaz, whose mother was Rahab..." And Rahab had a nick-name, didn't she? And do you know why Rahab is part of the story? It's because people like Rahab and Tamar and Judah and David and Matthew and you and me, we are the point of the story.

Chapter 4

"If I Can't Perform, How Does the Show Go On?"

When I was in seminary, I was required to take a number of counseling classes. In one of those classes I remember my professors saying that one of the primary causes of conflict in marriages stems from arguments over the "division of labor." That's a fancy way of saying, "Which task belongs to which person in a marriage?" Another way of saying it would be, "Who's responsible for what?" For example, if the trash isn't taken out or the dishes go unwashed or the floor doesn't get vacuumed, who's responsible? Now, this is pretty simple for most men to figure out because of the way we think. If it's outside, it's the man's responsibility. If it's inside, it's the woman's responsibility. You can't make it any simpler, but you would be amazed at the number of marriages that never figure this out.

In the same way, when it comes to living the Christian life, most Christians are confused about the division of labor. And it's because many Christians fall into the trap of thinking that salvation means that we get to go to Heaven when we die, and that's pretty much it. But salvation is so much more than Heaven. Salvation is the offer of life in God's Kingdom right here, right now, as well as after we die. It's about our lives being transformed now. In fact, this is what Paul wrote in Romans 8:28-29 about the topic: "And we know that in all things God works for the good of those who love him, who have been called according to his purpose. For those God foreknew he also predestined to be conformed to the image of his Son…" But many Christians are confused about the "division of labor" as it relates to the question, "Is spiritual transformation God's job or is it my job?"

And I'm sure that some of you hold to the position that spiritual transformation is solely God's job. In fact, your attitude is, "If I make any effort to be like Jesus, it just becomes legalism." And you'll even quote certain verses to defend your position like 1 Thessalonians 5:23-24: "May God himself, the God of peace, sanctify you through and through...The one who calls you is faithful, and he will do it." Or maybe you will refer to Romans 7:18: "For I know that good itself does not dwell in me, that is, in my sinful nature. For I have the desire to do what is good, but I cannot carry it out."

But there are others of you that take the Marine approach to your spiritual transformation as if it's the product of your commitment level. And you'll quote verses like Leviticus 11:44, "I am the Lord your God; consecrate yourselves and be holy, for I am holy." And your point is, "It's God's job to make sure He's holy and it's my job to make sure I'm holy." But when that happens, instead of a relationship, Christianity becomes a contest to see who can be the best Christian or who can memorize the most Bible verses or who can have the most faithful attendance to their small group, or who can pray the most and the longest, or who can read through their Bible in a year (including Leviticus). The problem is, when we live that way, we often develop a checklist mentality. We think things like, "As long as I'm doing these really good, even godly things, then I must be a good Christian."

By the way, that's the way I was raised. I grew up in North Carolina which is the belt buckle of the Bible Belt. And we were one of those families that was in church every time the doors were open. In fact, I'm pretty sure that my mom gave birth to me while she was singing in the soprano section of the choir because missing church for the birth a child would have never been an option. Growing up, we attended Sunday School every week. We attended Sunday Morning Worship service every week. We attended Sunday Evening Worship Service every week. We attended CTS (Bible study) every Sunday evening before the actual Sunday Evening Service every week. We attended Midweek Prayer Meeting every week. On Thursday evenings, we would meet at the church to get all jacked up and then we would go out into the community to ambush those who had visited the church the previous weekend with the goal of winning their lost souls for Jesus…every week. In other words, when it came to the church I grew up in, we were all in, all the time. By the way, as a side note for those of you that didn't grow up this way, the most dreaded words I ever heard growing up were: "We're going to have the opportunity to experience the blessing of having a revival." Now, if you didn't grow up in the South, you probably have no idea what a revival is. Well, a revival meant that we were going to be attending church, not just on Sunday and Wednesday and Thursday evenings, but we were going to get to attend every night that ended in "y" for an entire week. Some of you will figure that out in a few minutes and you will have a big belly laugh! But during revival week, a hired-gun evangelist would swing through town, and we would bribe all of our lost friends to attend church with us so that the evangelist could scare the hell out of them so they could go to Heaven when they died. I cannot count the number of times I heard the illustration about the Ferris Wheel of Hell that all lost sinners would be strapped into for all eternity as it went around and around and around. But the big finish that we all waited for as we sat beside our lost friends during that revival service was when the evangelist would talk about the weeping and the wailing and the gnashing of teeth that was the result of the pain that was going to be inflicted by the fire that was never going to be quenched and (drum roll, please) the worm that would never die! And when my friends would hear about that worm that refused to die, they would all rush down to the altar during one of the thirty-seven stanzas of, "Just as I am, without one plea" to make sure that they didn't end up on that Ferris Wheel of Hell with those creepy worms forever and ever and ever. Sure, it was scary, but it was definitely effective!

In fact, I'm sure that some of my friends suffered from such PTSD after attending one of our revival services that they were never able to attend the State Fair again just because of the memories that the Ferris Wheel brought back. My point is simply this: My life revolved around church. Our family never missed church due to a vacation or a weekend get-away. We never once had the discussion about whether or not we were going to church; it was a given; it was automatic. Church was our life. Church was my life. I was involved at every level. I taught Sunday School as a teenager. I sang in the choir. I was on the Bible Bowl team (which had absolutely nothing to do with bowling). I was a bus captain on Sunday mornings as we traveled around the community bribing children with candy to get on the bus so we could deliver them to church and then return them home afterwards. It was normal in those days, but I'll admit that it sounds kind of creepy now. As a result, on Sundays, I was at church before 7:00am and often not home until after 9:00 in the evening. My attitude was, "If God was going to be impressed with anyone, He was certainly going to be impressed with me!" And that approach was aided by the fact that the church I grew up in was all about performing...and I was a performer...and I was good at it. It was all about attending more, praying more, doing more and giving more. It was all about working harder and harder for the Kingdom. My approach to my relationship with God was, "It's my job to stay on God's good side and in His good graces, so I've got to try harder and run faster and pray longer and serve more; I can't slow down; I'll rest when I'm dead!" But is that what the Christian life is really all about? Is that really what Jesus had in mind when He said in John 10:10: "The thief comes only to steal and kill and destroy; I have come that they may have life and have it to the full."

Thankfully, in the Book of Philippians, Paul has some very important things to say about this business of the Christian life. For example, he said in Philippians 2:12-13: "…continue to work out your salvation with fear and trembling, for it is God who works in you to will and to act in order to fulfill his good pleasure." Notice the phrase, "…work out your own salvation." Paul is saying that when it comes to the Christian life, we play a role in the process. But then Paul goes on to say in Philippians 2:13: "…for it is God who is at work in you to will and to act in order to fulfill his good pleasure." In other words, although we are involved, we're not flying solo. Living the Christian life is empowered by God and it's impossible without Him, but we get to decide at what level we're going to participate. That's what Paul is talking about here. There's a role we play in our Christian journey, but we don't control it.

Now, having said that, one of my challenges as a pastor was having to speak every weekend to a whole lot of people who didn't really want to be in church, and you could divide those individuals into basically three groups. The first group was made up of people that didn't want to be in church because church just reminded them of how they were doing everything all wrong. And who wants to get all dressed up and show up to church just to be reminded that you are ticking God off?

The second group was made up of people who didn't like church because they didn't think they needed it. From their perspective, they had life wired; they already had it all together. Don't get me wrong, they would be the first to admit that they were no Billy Graham or Mother Teresa, but they were pretty sure that they weren't as bad as most people. They were just making their way through life trying to do their best while feeling good about the fact that they were at least average. They were thinking, "As long as God grades on the curve and accepts the A, B and C people and only rejects the D and F

people, I'm probably going to be okay." And, so, from their perspective, they didn't really need church.

The third group was made up of people who had been Christians for a long time, and that may describe you. But even
though that may describe you, you may still carry a sense of
shame and guilt because of something that you did, and as a result, you feel alienated and shut out by God. Or maybe it's because of a habit you're struggling with and you don't know what
to do about it. Or maybe, even worse, you don't want to do anything about it, and as a result, you feel like you must be on God's
naughty list. But if Jesus was standing before you right now, I
think He would say to you, "That's the whole problem with religion, because religion just muddies up the relationship you're
supposed to have with God."

By the way, do you know what religion is? Religion is our
attempt to work our way into a relationship with God. Religion
tells me that if I can be a good person and live by most of the
rules so that I get at least a C-, God and I are going to be okay.
But the problem with that logic is that we're not really sure
which rules we are supposed to live by.

For example, if we all made a list of what we consider to be
God's Top Five Rules, very few of us would agree on what
should be on that list. After all, we have all of the, "Thou shalt;
thou shalt not" rules from the Bible. And then we have the rules
we got from our parents like, "Don't smoke; don't drink; don't
chew (tobacco), and don't date girls who do." And then we have
rules that we've learned from organized religion that aren't even
in the Bible like, "You have to get your baby baptized and say
your hail Marys and sing the doxology and go through confir-
mation." And, so, we have all of these rules that we have to prioritize according to what we think is most important to God.
Which brings up the question, "Whose list of rules do we live
by?" For example, maybe a woman who had an abortion is high
on your list of things that you're pretty sure God hates. But in

your mind, your gossip about the woman who had the abortion isn't as big of a deal to God. Do you see how we prioritize? Do you get my point?

But not only do we prioritize, we also ignore the rules we're not good at obeying. For example, if you struggle with greed, you're pretty sure that giving generously to others who are in need isn't really that important to God. Why is that? It's because if we're not interested in obeying certain rules, it's easy for us to justify that those particular rules aren't really that big of a deal to God. If you struggle with pride, you can convince yourself that you're nowhere near as bad as someone who struggles with an addiction. You can just keep telling everyone what a humble servant you are and hopefully, eventually, they'll start believing you. My point is simply this: When it comes to living by rules, it gets very, very confusing. And that's why being a Christian isn't about following all the rules. It's about a relationship that's built on unconditional love. And whenever you interject a rule mind-set into a relationship that's built on unconditional love, you cancel out unconditional love. The two just don't mix.

Think about a relationship in your life that's based on your performance. Let me ask you a question: How secure are you in that relationship? For example, take your job. If you don't do your job at work, you're out. Your boss doesn't say at your annual review, "You haven't sold a thing in seven years, but we sure like having you around." It doesn't work that way. If you don't perform, you are history. Everyone may love you. Everyone may want to go to lunch with you. Everyone may appreciate your fruitcake at Christmas, but if you don't perform, you're out. And so, there's an element of insecurity in that relationship.

It's also true in some marriages. For some of you, the security in your marriage is based on how you perform and if you meet certain expectations. And when you don't perform or meet those expectations, you feel like a loser. You feel alienated and condemned. Why is that? It's because that's the nature of performance-oriented relationships. Performance destroys the relationship by canceling out unconditional love. And since that's how it is in our relationships with each other, we naturally look at God and think, "He must be the same way with us!" But if that's the case, we're in trouble because we know deep down inside that we're not measuring up. We know that if the key to having a relationship with God is based on getting all the rules right all the time, we're on the outside looking in.

But the good news about Christianity is that our Heavenly Father operates on a completely different system – and that's what this chapter is all about. We're going to learn how to actually experience the life that Jesus died for us to experience.

Paul said this is Romans 8, and it lays the foundation for this entire chapter. Romans 8:1: "Therefore, there is now no condemnation (none, zilch, zero) for those who are really doing their very, very best to live by God's rules." Fooled you; that's not what it says, but let's be honest, that's how most of us live our lives. It actually says in Romans 8:1: "Therefore, there is now no condemnation for those who are in Christ Jesus." Do you know what that means? It means that when you become a Christian, there's nothing that can come between you and God, not even your sin. It means that you're *uncondemnable* (and I'm not sure that's a real word, but I'm now declaring it one). Let me give you a definition for condemn: "To pronounce an unfavorable or adverse judgment on; to express strong disapproval of..." Why is that important? It's important because many of us as Christians feel that when we break one of God's rules, God disapproves of us. But Paul tells us in Romans 8:1 that once we become a Christian, God never disapproves of us; He never condemns us. In fact, if you are in Christ, you are *uncondemnable*. But that's not all there is to the definition: condemn: "To pronounce an unfavorable or adverse judgment on, to express strong disapproval of; to pronounce guilty, to judge or to pronounce unfit for use or service." Maybe you're reading this and you're just coming off of an affair. I guarantee you, because of the Christian culture we live in, you feel like there's something uniquely wrong about your struggle. And unless I miss my guess, you feel condemned; you feel unfit for use or service. But I want you to know that if you've trusted Jesus Christ as your personal Savior, you're as in as Billy Graham, because it isn't about what you did or what you're doing. It's about, "Have you trusted in Jesus Christ as your personal Savior?"

And right now, some of you are thinking, "Whoa…Mike you're on a slippery slope. You mean to tell me that there's no condemnation even if you kill somebody or if you commit suicide?" Not if you've trusted in Jesus Christ as your personal Savior. And right now, some of you who've been around church for a while are thinking about throwing this book in the trash! And it's because this way of thinking is so strange to us, even to those of us who've followed Jesus for years, that we freak out when we hear something like this. And the reason is because, for many of us, we were saved by grace through faith; we were saved by trusting Jesus. But then, a couple of hours later, we reverted back to the old system of behavior. And we went right back to following a bunch of rules because we're convinced that it's our job to please God and to be what God wants us to be. But Paul writes to the Christians at Rome and tells them: "If you're in Christ, there is no condemnation. If you're in Christ, sin has lost its power to separate you relationally from your Heavenly Father." And that means that when we sin, God doesn't turn his back on us. He doesn't flinch. He's not shocked. He doesn't even roll his eyes, because we are "in Christ Jesus."

And Paul explains why in Romans 8:2: "…because through Christ Jesus the law of the Spirit who gives life has set you free from the law of sin and death." This is what Paul is saying. He's saying that we are used to a philosophy that says, "You've got to get it right if you're going to be in a relationship with God, and if you're ever going to get it all together." We're used to:

"You've got to be good and do good and obey all the rules." And that's what Paul refers to in Romans 8:2 as "the law (or system) of sin and death." Its cause and effect: "You sin; you die – you blow it, you're out!" And that's the system we're all born into; that's the system that we are used to. And, so, it makes sense that when we read the Bible and see all of the rules, we naturally do our best to obey them, but we can't. But Paul comes along and tells us that the reason we're not condemned when we break the rules is because God introduced a whole new system. You can see it in Romans 8:2: "…the law of the Spirit who gives life." And this new system is the total opposite of the system we're used to, because in this new system you're not "in" based on what you do, and you don't "stay in" based on what you do. You're "in" because of what Jesus did, period! It's a completely different system. And even though both of the systems are in operation, the new system overrides the old system. Let me see if I can explain it. We are all familiar with the Law of Gravity. The Law of Gravity means that when you drop an object, it will fall to the ground. But have you ever thought while sitting on a plane awaiting take off, "There's no way this plane should get off the ground!" Ponder this: the weight of a fully loaded Boeing 747-400 Jumbo Jet is 910,000 pounds. That's the equivalent of 325 double decker buses! But what happens? The engines roar and the plane accelerates, and seconds later, you are in the air defying the Law of Gravity.

Now, I'll let you in on a secret. You can drop this book a million times and it will fall to the floor a million times. You will never get it to pause in the air. However, you can get on a plane that weighs almost 500 tons and fill it with hundreds of people along with all of their luggage, and as long as there's fuel, you can fly all day. How is that possible? Did something happen to the Law of Gravity? No! Then what's the difference? It's because there's an overriding system; it's the Law of Aerodynamics.

In the same way, God says to us, "You're very familiar with

the old system; you're very familiar with the law of sin and death. You know what that's all about. In fact, you've spent your entire life operating by that system. It affects how you treat people and how they treat you." But God wants us to understand that Christianity is not a version of the old system. Christianity is a whole different thing. And Paul explains why in Romans 8:3: "For what the law was powerless to do because it was weakened by the flesh…" Do you know what that means? It means that the Law didn't work because no one could keep the Law! Paul says that the law or the system of trying to please God by obeying all of the just rules doesn't work; it's powerless. It's powerless when it comes to getting to God and it's powerless when it comes to walking with God. Why is that? It's because the system of doing our best and trying harder and keeping all the rules is based entirely on our ability to perform. But God comes along and says, "You've already flunked performance. You can't perform well enough to please me." So, what we couldn't do in our effort and strength, God did for us! And that's the fundamental building block of Christianity.

So, what did God do? You can read about it in Romans 8:3: "For what the law was powerless to do because it was weakened by the flesh, God did by sending his own Son in the likeness of sinful flesh to be a sin offering." In other words, what the Law couldn't do, God, through Jesus, did. Let me put it another way: Where the law was impotent, God was omnipotent. God didn't condemn you and me. Instead, God condemned sin.

What does that mean to us? It means that once we're in Christ, our sin can never separate us from God again. Think about that! God never puts us on probation. He doesn't establish boundaries. He never says, "I'm keeping an eye on you until you can prove to me that you have your act together." Why is that? It's because God overpowered the cause and effect, sin and death relationship. Now, trust me on this, it's still operating (and we'll see that in just a few pages). But God says, "In me, it's overcome." In fact, Paul goes on to say in Romans 8:4 that it was done in order that "the righteous requirement of the law might be fully met in us." Do you know what the requirement of the law was? The requirement of the law was perfection. And, so God says, "Once you are in Christ, I am giving it to you…you can't earn it…you can't achieve it… you can't perform enough… I am giving you righteousness and perfection; I'm crediting it to your account." And if you're like me, you read that and think, "I don't act very righteous!" But that's okay because it's the old system. In this new system, God says that when we are in Christ, He credits to our lives all the righteousness and all the perfection of Jesus Christ. And that means that when God looks at you and me, He sees us as righteous as His own Son, Jesus, because we are in Him, and now, He wants us to operate our lives from that position. He doesn't want us to revert back to, "God is mad at me because I looked at porn, but I had twelve quiet times and so I should be okay for a while." Or "I'm on God's bad side because I was envious of my neighbor's new car. But I went to my small group five weeks in a row and so I should be good now." When we revert to that way of thinking, God is like, "Stop it; that's religion; that's a performance mentality; that's the old system, and my Son had to die to overcome that system. And through His death I've given you the gift of righteousness. You are righteous; you're not condemnable. In fact, there's not a thing you can do to alter my love and my acceptance of you."

By the way, there are a lot of Christians who really, really love God, but they have areas in their lives that don't line up with the character of God. We all have areas that don't fall in the line with the person that God has called us to be. And as a result, in that area of our lives, we don't resemble God. And one of the ways you can identify this kind of sin in your life is that you do a pretty good job of keeping it hidden until you're stressed. But when stress comes, you're in trouble. It's like a pot of gold. What happens when the heat is turned up under a pot of gold? The impurities come to the top. That's how you purify gold. When the impurities come to the surface of the gold, the impurities are skimmed off. In the same way, if you're a Christian, from God's perspective, you are gold. But sometimes the heat gets turned up in our lives and, just like with gold, impurities come to the surface. And when that happens, we often wonder: "Where did that come from?" Well, it's probably a sin that we're in bondage to that has been holding us captive. And what's amazing is that the sin is usually totally out of character to who we really are. But when we have these moments, this is what Satan will do: Satan will say, "That's who you really are." So, when those moments come, this is your response to Satan: "That's not who I really am; I'm righteous, I'm perfect; I'm a new creation in Jesus." 2 Corinthians 5:17 says, "Therefore, if anyone is in Christ, the new creation has come: The old has gone, the new is here!" In other words, "I'm a new creation in Jesus, but I still have some areas in my life that I'm dealing with."

David is a great example. The Bible says that David was a man after God's own heart. That statement isn't made about any other person in the Bible, but it was made about David, not once, but twice. But in just a matter of a few days, he commits adultery and murder. It was totally out of his character. And when he confessed his sin, this is what he said in Psalm 51:12: "Restore to me the joy of your salvation." He didn't say: "Restore my salvation." And I point that out because I want you to understand that when you blow it, God doesn't kick you out of His family. He still sees you as righteous. He still sees you as perfect. And it's because our salvation isn't based on what we do or don't do, or we would all be in trouble. Our salvation is based on Jesus' righteousness and what He did for us on the cross. And as a result, we are secure in His power and His grace.

Think about it this way. When it comes to our relationship with God, it's really no different than the relationship we have with our children. I have two sons. When they blow it, how does it factor into my behavior and feelings toward them? The answer is, "zero, zilch, nada!" It doesn't matter because they're my sons. And no matter what they do, we'll still be as tight and as close as we've ever been, because they're my sons. And in the same way, when God looks at you and me, he says, "I don't care what you've done; there is no condemnation; there is no separation; you're my child." Do you know what that means? It means that there's not a sliver of sin that can slide in between you and God that can alter his love and acceptance for you. And it's because you didn't get into a relationship with God by being good, and He doesn't love you because you're staying good. He loves you because you were declared righteous when you received His Son as your Savior, and as a result, there's no potential for condemnation.

Now, if you've never received Jesus as your Savior, I have some good news and bad news. The bad news is that you are condemned, but it's not because of anything you've done. It's because you, like me, was also born into a world that says you have to perform, and that's all it takes to be condemned — just being born. The good news is that you can be reborn. And you can be taken out of a state of condemnation and placed into a state of total acceptance by God. All you have to do is accept this gift of righteousness. All you have to do is to receive the gift of Jesus Christ and accept Him as your Savior. In other words, you take whatever you are trusting in to be in a good standing with God and you transfer that trust to what Jesus has already done for you. You accept that His death on the cross paid for all of your sins. And when you accept it, God stamps across your life, "Righteous." But for that to happen, you have to get to the point where you can say, "God, I can't do anything to make me perfect and righteous. I'm helpless and I'm hopeless! I don't need a second chance; I need a Savior. I don't need to try harder; I need a Savior. I need someone to do for me what I can't do for myself." And once we appropriate that to our lives by trusting in Jesus as our personal Savior, we become *uncondemnable*. And we are as accepted and close to God as we can possibly be. We are, at that moment, positionally perfect. But it isn't because of anything we've done; it's because of what Christ has done for us. That's the new system that God put into place through Jesus.

But our tendency is to see this new system in Christ as only relating to us getting into Heaven when we die, but we don't understand how it applies to our lives now. But the good news is that the "Spirit who gives life" has as much to do with life now as it does with going to Heaven when we die. Jesus didn't say,"I've come that you might go to Heaven." Jesus said in John 10:10, "I've come that you might have life and have it to the full." That means that the Christian experience isn't just about going to Heaven when we die. The option of a full life begins at the moment of our salvation. And I know what some of you are thinking right now: "But I don't understand how it works!" And that's okay because this is a truth that you will begin to understand as you grow in your Christian walk, but it's also a truth that you need to start taking advantage of now because it's just as true now whether you understand not or not, and it's true because it comes from God's word. And so let's unpack this truth.

Let's assume that when you became a Christian, you already had a sense of right and wrong. You already knew that it was bad to kill people and kick the neighbor's dog. You already knew that you were supposed to take care of the environment. You already knew that you were supposed to be a good employee and parent and spouse and neighbor. But then one day you realized that no matter how good you are, you will never be good enough to restore your relationship with God. But you also discovered that Jesus, because of His grace, is willing to forgive you of your sin now, and as a result, you get to go to Heaven when you die. That's a great deal! But you always assumed, because it just makes sense, that you're still supposed to be good and obey all the rules. And that doesn't really bother you because you once heard a preacher say that if you obey all of the rules, it will change your marriage and your family and your relationships; it will even change your finances. So, you take off on your Christian journey assuming that everything hinges on how you perform and behave. But what happens when we do that? All we have done is taken the old system where we thought we could somehow please God and earn his love, and we've dressed it up with religious stuff. And when we do that, we revert right back to the old system: "My job is to work really hard to be a good Christian and obey all of the rules." And what's amazing is that there is a small group of people that can actually pull it off. There are some Christians who are just naturally disciplined and structured. They're naturally good rule keepers; in fact, they were good rule keepers before they became Christians. And so when they accept the gift of salvation and begin to walk with Jesus, they memorize the whole Bible. They never miss church. They give generously. They volunteer in their community. They pray without ceasing. They refuse to gossip. They don't judge others. They do all of the things they assume you need to do to be a good Christian. And we look at that kind of person from a distance and think, "That's the best Christian I have ever seen in my life." But if you actually get close to that individual and peel back the layers, you might discover that this is a person who decided, "I'm going to be a good Christian even if it kills me!" And if you spend enough time with them, it won't take long before you begin to see through the facade. And don't get me wrong, they are sincere. They are doing what they think they're supposed to be doing. But do you know how you can spot this kind of person? They usually have a judgmental side to them. Now, they won't see it as judgmental; they will see it as discernment. But you don't want to get too close because not only do they think they are perfect, they also think you should be perfect. And they have no problem telling you what you need to do to make that happen, And we all know people like that and we do our best to avoid them.

But my guess is that most of you are more like me. You have also tried to manhandle the Christian life and it lasted about three weeks before you blew it in some way. And then you felt incredibly guilty and so you went through the whole rededication routine. You prayed, "God, I'm so sorry I blew it and I'll never blow it again, and this time I really, really mean it. Last time I only really meant it but this time I'm serious. I'm sold out; this time I'm all in!"

And you start reading your Bible and you get back involved with your small group and it feels like things are going great. But then one day while you are reading your Bible, you come across a verse like Ephesians 5:22: "Wives, submit to your husbands..." And you're like, "God are you serious; have you met my husband?" Or you come across the verse where we are told to give cheerfully. And you read that and think, "God, you've got to be kidding?" "Control my thought life; never lust; never gossip? Respect those in authority over me?" And all of a sudden, you're like, ,"God, I'll try, but don't get your hopes up." And so we give it our best shot, but we fail. And we respond, "God, I'm sorry; I'll try harder next time. I'll get counseling. I'm sure this has something to do with my childhood and the fact that I never had a puppy. I'm going to figure out how to live the Christian life!"

But here's a truth that maybe no one has ever told you: You can't live the Christian life, in fact, you were never expected to. And as long as your attitude is, "God, thanks for the rules and guidelines; I'll take it from here," you will always fail because you cannot live the Christian life. In fact, do you know what the Christian life is? The Christian life is Christ's life, and you can't imitate Him.

I just watched the Winter Olympics. I used to be an avid snow skier. I skied Mammoth, Heavenly, even Squaw Valley where the 1960 Olympics were held, but there's no way I could ever ski like an Olympian. In fact, there is no way I could ever do anything those athletes can do, except maybe curling. I think that maybe I could crush curling. My point is, if I can't imitate people like that, how am I going to imitate Jesus? The Christian life is the life of Christ and that's why it's called the Christian life. It's not called the disciplined life. It's not called the holy life. It's not called the righteous life. It's called the Christian life; it's His life. And the only person who ever lived the Christian life was Christ.

And so the reason that we keep lusting and gossiping and lying and losing our temper is because God didn't leave us here in this system to conquer those things. That's why Jesus came to this earth. He came to conquer those things so that we might have life, His life. The standard of holiness and righteousness wasn't given as a goal for us to try and achieve so that we can make ourselves better. The Christian life isn't a self-improvement program. The Christian life is the life of Jesus. And the goal isn't simply to make ourselves better so we can earn some gold stars by our name. The goal is to allow Jesus Christ to live His life through us.

Now, the Bible has a term for the old approach to living the Christian life. It's called, "living according to the flesh." That's simply a reference to you and me taking our best shot in our own strength at trying to build a relationship with God. But Romans 8:3-4 says, "For what the law was powerless to do because it was weakened by the flesh, God did by sending his own Son in the likeness of sinful flesh to be a sin offering. And so He condemned sin in the flesh, in order that the righteous requirement of the law might be fully met in us, who do not live according to the flesh but according to the Spirit." So, Paul says, "Those of us who are Christians don't live according to the flesh." Why not? Well, since we have the Spirit of Christ, we live our lives prompted by the Spirit of Christ. And He doesn't live inside of us just because it's warm and cozy. He lives inside of us to direct our lives.

Now, compare that to the way I was raised with all of the legalism and rules. When you live in that system, you are constantly focused on your sin. And so you sin and then you feel guilty about the sin, and so you confess the sin. But before long, you sin again and you start the whole cycle all over. And so the problem with that system is that you are conscious of your sin all of the time. And as a result, you focus on your sin and you make plans for it. You are even prepared so that when the sin occurs, you're ready to confess it and deal with it. Sometimes you even confess it while you're doing it. Don't act like you have never done that. But that's "living in the flesh" and that's never what God intended the Christian life to be.

Let me give you a definition for "living in the flesh": "Trusting in my strength and determination to bring about whatever changes I feel need to take place." It's, "God, now that I'm a Christian, I'm going to be a better spouse or boss or employee or parent or child (you fill in the blank)." And you mean it, and you feel it, you just can't do it. But don't feel bad, because neither can I…or anyone else. And it's because we don't have the strength or the power or the discipline. We don't have what it takes to live the Christian life. Here's the second part of that definition for "living in the flesh": "Retaining control of my life, giving primary consideration to my needs, desires, appetites, and fears when making decisions." Let me put it another way: "God, this is what I'm willing to do, but this is what I'm not willing to do." For example, you are more than willing to follow Jesus, but you want to follow Him on your own terms. And so, your attitude is, "This is where I'll go and this is what I'll do and this is what I'm willing to give up, but this is where I'm not willing to go and this is what I'm not willing to do, and this is what I'm not willing to give up." But that approach to life, whether you're a Christian or not, leads to the same place. Paul describes it in Romans 8:6: "The mind governed by the flesh is death…" Don't forget what we've learned about the old system: Wherever there is sin, there's death. Sin and death are always attached. In fact, whatever sin touches, it dies. That's "living according to the flesh," and it always leads to death because you can't Just. Not. Sin. You're just not that good or strong or disciplined, and it's because you're not Jesus. But I lived most of my life that way. And I'll never forget the moment I came to the conclusion, "I can't do this; I'm just not that good!" And God was like, "Finally! What do you think I've been trying to tell you for all of these years?" And even though I spent my life feeling like a failure because I couldn't live the Christian life, I wasn't a failure; I was just normal. Because the only person who can live the Christian life is Jesus, and that's why God had to develop this new system. Because in this new system, you can experience the life of Jesus through you.

When you get right down to it, it's finishing the race the way we started the race. It's not, "Thank you God for saving me; I'll take it from here." It's, "God, I'm just as helpless as I was when I faced life and eternity without any hope, and I'm still that helpless when it comes to being the person I ought to be. I'm just as helpless when it comes to my pride. I'm just as helpless when it comes to dealing with lust. I'm just as helpless when it comes to dealing with gossip. I'm weak and I need a Savior." That is the first step to experiencing the Christian life. It's realizing that we finish the way we started. We need the righteousness of Christ to assure us life in Heaven and we need the righteousness of Christ to assure us victory over sin Monday through Sunday. It's not our strength or dedication or discipline; in fact, it has nothing to do with me and you. It's, "God, I can't, but you can." "I can't be the spouse you need me to be today, but you can." "I can't be the employee you need to be today, but you can." "I can't overcome the temptations in my life, but you can." But for that to happen, you have to give up the fight, and you've got to come to a place in your life where you say, "I give up because I just can't do it." And God says, "Great, now we're getting somewhere." And it will change your experience as a Christian as Christ lives through you because only Jesus can live the life of Christ. Sure, we have a lot of principles and rules and precepts that we need to learn to obey, but the context for all of that is, "I can't, but He can."

Chapter 5

"Love Will Keep Us Together!"

When it comes to relationships in our culture, whether we realize it or not, there are three basic ways that we approach them: We convince; we manipulate, and we control. In other words, if we can learn how to convince people that we are right, and if we can learn how to manipulate those individuals through guilt and circumstances, we can learn how to control them so we get our way. And if that happens, we assume that we will be successful in our relationships. After all, we will get what we want out of the relationship and that means we will be happy. And we may not do it consciously, but that's the way we tend to operate. That's the way we operate when we're in a marriage that's on the rocks. That's the way we operate when we're dealing with a prodigal son or daughter. That's the way we operate with our roommate that's getting on our last nerve; we convince, manipulate and control. And the reason we approach our relationships this way is because we all believe that we are the one that's right and balanced. That's why we think things like, "If everybody else was more like me, it would be a better world." Or, "If my spouse was more like me, we'd have a better marriage." Or, "If my kids were more like me, we'd have a better family." Whether we want to admit it or not, we have a tendency to think that way. We naturally assume that if everyone would just see the world the way we see it, the world would be a better place and we'd all be happy. And as a result, we naturally tend to gravitate to the people who agree with us and we also tend to avoid those who disagree with us. We love the people who love us in return. We accept the people who accept us in return because it benefits us to do relationships that way. But then Jesus comes along and messes up everything by saying in Matthew 5:43-44: "You have heard that it was said, 'Love your neighbor and hate your enemy.' But I tell you, love your enemies and pray for those who persecute you..." To which my natural response is, "No offense, Jesus, but I have a hard enough time consistently loving the people who love and accept me. I have a hard enough time consistently loving the people that have my back. And so for you to set the expectation that I'm supposed to love my enemies, that's just taking this Christian thing too far!"

But what we're going to learn in this chapter is that what Jesus taught about relationships is totally opposite of everything we've ever believed about relationships. And we're also going to learn that how we handle our relationships is so much a part of Jesus' agenda for those of us who follow Him, it's going to take us some time for it to really sink in. And all of us are going to have to re-evaluate the way we approach our relationships, because Jesus basically says, "If you only love the people who love you and accept you and agree with you, you're no better than the tax collectors." We talked about the whole tax collector thing earlier when we talked about Matthew, and so I'm sure this Jewish audience was like, "Oooh, low blow," because in Jesus' day every Jew hated tax collectors. But Jesus's point was, "Anybody can love and accept the people that love and accept them, but I have a different standard; I want you to love your enemies." And that makes us uncomfortable because we can't see how that is going to benefit us. Plus, that's so different from what we're used to. As I said earlier, we're used to loving and accepting the people that love and accept us, but we've also learned that it's in our best interest to kiss up to some people we can't stand if it somehow benefits us in the long run. We're even willing to say we're sorry for something that's not our fault if it somehow benefits us. That's how most of us approach our relationships. We love and accept the people who love and accept us, and then we learn how to tolerate the people we can't stand if we think it will somehow benefit us. But then Jesus comes along and says to those of us who follow Him, "That doesn't make you any different than the people who don't follow me; everybody does that." And then, as if that's not enough, Jesus continues in Matthew 5:47: And if you greet (the word means, "to hold in honor, esteem") only your own people, what are you doing more than others? Do not even pagans do that?" Allow me to interpret what Jesus is saying. He's saying, "I expect more out of you than I expect out of everybody else." In other words, for Christians, there's a different standard for how we approach our relationships. There's a higher calling. Those who don't follow Jesus can get by with simply being nice to the people who are nice to them in return. They can get by tolerating an individual they can't stand if that relationship benefits them. But for those of us who have made the decision to follow Jesus, the standard is higher. We are called to also love the person who makes our life miserable.

And then Jesus concludes his thoughts in Matthew 5:48: "Be perfect, therefore, as your Heavenly Father is perfect." And we read that and our immediate response is, "That's impossible," but let me explain what this verse is saying. It's saying that the closest we will ever get to perfection in this life is when we treat our enemies with kindness, respect and love. That's the ultimate act of godliness. Let me say it another way: The closest we will ever come to being like God is when we love our enemies. Godliness has nothing to do with the amount of Bible knowledge we have. It has nothing to do with the number of deep and profound books we read; it's all about our ability to love. And so Jesus says, "If your goal is to be like your Father in Heaven, then you're going to have to learn to love the way He loves. Like Father, like child."

So, Jesus has an agenda for each of us, and it's not the agenda that we would choose because never once does Jesus make our benefit the end all of a relationship; He has a completely different agenda. And His agenda is that we extend grace and acceptance and love to our enemies the very same way that grace and acceptance and love has been extended to us. And as His hands and feet on his earth, we are the biggest hypocrites in the world if we think we can share the message of God's unconditional forgiveness and acceptance and love, and yet, we're conditional in our forgiveness and acceptance and love. We're the biggest phonies in the world if we're telling people, "You ought to become a Christian! It doesn't matter what you've done or how bad you've blown it," but then we refuse to love our enemies. There's something tragically wrong with a church where the message is a message of unconditional love and acceptance and grace to people who don't deserve it when, as individuals, we aren't willing to dispense that same unconditional love and acceptance and grace to one another.

So, who's the person in your life that you have the most difficult time getting along with? Who's the person who's always on your case? Who's the person that you think has an agenda to ruin you? Jesus says, "That's your target; now learn to love that person because you are the instrument through which I want to communicate unconditional grace, acceptance and love." And it's not so that we will get along better with people. It's not so that our lives will be easier. It's because it's the mission that God has given us as Christians.

And I believe that one of the biggest reasons that the church has lost some of its effectiveness in our society today is because we have adopted the pagan's standard for relationships. In other words, when it comes to our family, or spouse, or boss, or employees, or friends or neighbors it's all about convincing, manipulating and controlling. But when we talk about Jesus, we talk about unconditional love and grace and acceptance and forgiveness. Do you see how that could send a mixed message?

So, Jesus said to this Jewish audience that was living in a culture where they were beaten down everyday by their Roman occupiers, "This is where I'm taking you if you choose to follow me; I want you to love your persecutors and your enemies." Here's the idea: Think of what would happen in your marriage, or with your prodigal son or daughter, or with your parent, or friend, or coworker, or roommate, or neighbor, or with that relative that keeps borrowing money but never pays you back if you consciously said, "My role in their life is not to convince them of anything, or to manipulate them into doing what I think they should do; my role in their life isn't to control them. My calling is to love them and leave the convincing, manipulating and controlling to God." What would happen in that relationship?

And right now, some of you are already thinking of reasons why you can't love this way. You're thinking, "But they don't deserve it!" Or, "You don't know my story!" Or, "The situation is too emotionally charged; there's too much hurt and pain!" Or, "If I love that way, I feel like they would be getting away with what they did!" Or, "If I love that way, they would just run all over me and take advantage of me!" Just so you know, God could have used all of those excuses on us. "They don't deserve it; they're sinful, rotten people!" Or, "The idea of my Son dying on a cross for them is too emotionally charged; I just can't do that." Or, "If I save these people, it's like they're getting away with their bad behavior." Or, "If I save these people, they're just going to run all over me." Before you go there, you need to realize that every time you sin you're basically saying, "God, thank you for your Son and thank you for your salvation. Now I get to do what I want and I still get to go to Heaven when I die." But keep this in mind, every time we sin, we throw God's goodness and grace up in his face. But do you know what he says? He says, "I'm going to love my enemies and treat those who are unfriendly to me as friends because that's what I'm like."

If we are really interested in following Jesus, our Heavenly
Father is going to lead us to love our enemies so we can be like
his sons and daughters. It's so we can be authentic dispensers
of unconditional love, grace and forgiveness. And we don't have
to go there, but that's where He's going to lead us. But if we'll
let Him, do you know what He'll do? He'll lead us over the hur-
dle of what those people do deserve and don't deserve. He'll
lead us through the barrier of all the emotion that's attached to
the situation. He'll lead us over the mountain of our fear of being
taken advantage of, and He'll lead us through the wall of what
we think they deserve. He'll deal with all of that. But I want to
warn you, if you're interested in handling relationships the way
God wants you to handle relationships, He's going to lead you
to love your enemies.

Now, before you decide that you're going to put this book
down and never pick it up again, let me ask you a question: How
would you like to be married to someone who refused to convince, manipulate and control you, and, instead, they just loved
you unconditionally? That's different isn't it? I mean, we don't
want to be that way, but we would love to be married to someone like that? Wouldn't it be great to have a parent that, instead
of trying to convince, manipulate and control you, just loved
you? Wouldn't it be great to have kids like that? Wouldn't it be
great to have friends like that? You see, when we turn it around,
it's no-brainer, and that's where God wants to take all of us.
Imagine what could happen in a local church if we could begin
to really love this way? Imagine what could happen on a church
staff? Imagine what could happen in our communities. The
question is, "What does it really mean to have God's love for one
another; how do we live that out?" These questions aren't as
easy to answer as you might think. And it didn't help either
when I looked into what Jesus said to His disciples in John 13:34:
"A new command I give you: Love one another. As I have loved
you, so you must love one another." Notice that it's a command-

ment, not a suggestion. And the commandment isn't that we love God; it's that we love one another.

And then Jesus gives us his drop the-mic line in John 13:35: "By this everyone will know that you are my disciples, if you love one another." And I read that and think, "That's why our neighbors don't know that we're followers of Jesus." They know that we go to church, but I'm not sure that they really know what a Christian is. Why is that? Well, somehow the church has lost that magnetic appeal of love. That explains why a stranger can walk into a church and feel unwelcome and unwanted. It's because he or she doesn't sense the love relationship among us and, as a result, they walk away and often never return. Do you know why? It's because people are not persuaded; they're attracted.

Paul wrote something that is very practical when it comes to this topic in Romans 12:9-10: "Love must be sincere. Hate what is evil; cling to what is good. Be devoted to one another in love. Honor one another above yourselves." Notice that phrase, "Be devoted to one another in love." We're getting ready to look at that great treatise on the topic of love that Paul wrote in 1 Corinthians 13. The Greek word that Paul used in 1 Corinthians 13 for love is that familiar word, *agape* (from the Greek, agápē). And Paul often used this word throughout his letters. But the word for love that Paul uses in Romans 12:9 is the Greek word, *phileo*. It means, "brotherly love" or, "to be devoted to one another in affection." Paul also wrote in Romans 15:7: "Accept one another, then, just as Christ accepted you." The word accept was used frequently in two very significant ways in the days of Paul. First, it was used in reference to accepting someone into your home. For example, when your friend comes to your door, you invite them in; you receive them. You don't carry on a lengthy conversation while they're standing on the porch. There is acceptance, or there should be. The word accept was also used in the context of a military unit; a soldier was accepted into the unit.

In other words, there was one accord. That's what accept means. All of this is involved in this idea of fellowship within the church family. In fact, it was that intimacy of fellowship that kept the church strong when it was bleeding and hurting during the days of persecution.

Now, to be totally honest, this chapter kicked my butt while I was writing it. Every stroke I made on my keyboard reminded me of just how short I fall in this area of my life. As I have often told a close friend of mine, I'm a work in progress, but it felt like I underwent open heart surgery as I wrote this chapter. And so, I'm probably going to bleed all over you as we visit the operating room where God has been working in my life. It is in 1 Corinthians 13 where we learn to actually love the way that Jesus has called us to love. We can sit around in our small groups and talk about the "what" all day long, but we need to figure out the "how." We need to talk about the involvements and the risks. We need to discover the specific details of what this kind of love entails, and thankfully, God has given us a very clear map.

Paul begins 1 Corinthians 13 by addressing the priority of love, and he gives us five conditional clauses, and then Paul follows each of these conditional clauses with three identical statements. 1 Corinthians 13:1-3: "If I speak in the tongues of men or of angels, but do not have love, I am only a resounding gong or a clanging cymbal. If I have the gift of prophecy and can fathom all mysteries and all knowledge, and if I have a faith that can move mountains, but do not have love, I am nothing. If I give all I possess to the poor and give over my body to hardship that I may boast, but do not have love, I gain nothing."

When a writer in the Bible repeats something, he's doing it to for emphasis; he's doing it to get your attention. And so Paul is trying to drive home a very simple, direct point. He's saying, "If I do the most impressive things known to man, even martyrdom, but I don't have love, the outcome is nothing, zero, zilch." In other words, we can knock ourselves out as Christians. We can enter into worship. We can give generously. We can attend our small group. We can pray and study the Bible. We can go through all the motions, but if there isn't love, as far as God is concerned, it means nothing.

Now, if we're going to unpack this topic of love, it's essential that we understand what the word really means. As I mentioned earlier, the word that Paul uses here for love is the Greek word, agape, which means, "seeking the highest good of the other person." It's not an emotional love, although it will always involve the emotions. The source of this love is the mind. There is a mental decision that is consciously made to seek the highest good of the other person, and to do that requires that we think more about the other person than we think about ourselves, and that's where it gets tough. In fact, in the next few verses, Paul gives us fifteen characteristics of this kind of love. And this may seem a little bit like a seminary crash course, but I want us to work our way through the characteristics one by one.

1st: "Love is patient." What does it mean to be patient? We have an English colloquialism, "short tempered," but we don't have a word for "long-tempered," however, that's what the word patient really means. The Greek word is *makrothyméō*, and the first part of the word means long or far in the distance, while the latter part of the word means heat. The Greek word for heat is *thumos*; we get our word thermometer from it. The thought is this: "long before we get heated." For example, it's a word that was used in the first century to describe a person who had been wronged and he had the ability to avenge himself, but he didn't. That's this word; that's patience.

Another thing I discovered is that whenever this translated word, patience, is used in the New Testament, it's always used in reference to people. The word endurance is used in relation to circumstances. For example, if you're in a hurry and you discover that you have a flat tire, in the New Testament sense, you endure that, but you're not patient with it. You're patient with people. What Paul is saying is, "Your patient response to people reveals your love." Let me say it another way: If there isn't patience, there isn't love.

Now let's be honest; we really aren't patient people. I'm sure you've heard the American's prayer, "Lord give me patience, and I want it right now." That's the way we are. But God says, "You want patience? Fine, I'll help you with your patience." And He brings seventeen interruptions into your life before noon to help you in that process. Have you ever experienced that? We all have. Love is patient.

2nd: "Love is kind." The Greek word *chrēsteuetai* translated into kind means helpful. It also means free from petty criticism. It's the idea of having a positive spirit; there's even a sense of friendliness connected with this word. It's the same word that's used in the Bible for wine that's aged until it becomes mellow. Jesus used this word in Matthew 11:30, "My yoke is easy." In other words, it's not harsh; it's pleasant and kind.

It reminded me of what we saw earlier in the story of the woman caught in adultery. Do you remember Jesus' approach? After all of the woman's accusers had dropped their rocks and walked away, Jesus looked at her and said, "Where are those that condemn you? I don't condemn you either, Now, go and sin no more." Was he kind or was he unkind? He was kind and he was gentle.

Let's be honest, if most of us would have been there that day, we would have been looking for a rock instead of asking, "How can I help?" Asking to help is kindness. And Paul says that if we don't have this type of love, we can talk a good game until we are blue in the face, but there will never be harmony or restoration in our relationships. There's no way that we can be involved in meeting each other's needs if there is a critical spirit that says, "Why can't you get your act together?" Love is kind.

3rd: "Love does not envy." Some versions of the Bible translate this phrase, "Love is not jealous." And I think that's appropriate because jealousy and envy are in the same family, but there is a difference. Jealousy is the inordinate passion for me to keep what I have. Envy is the inordinate passion for me to acquire what you have; that's the difference. Jealousy wants to keep. Envy wants to get. There's a small part of a verse in the Song of Solomon 8:6 that says, "Jealousy is as severe as the grave." Love does not envy.

And now, as if the passage hasn't been hard enough on us, Paul goes on to say in 1 Corinthians 13:4-5: "…it does not boast, it is not proud. It does not dishonor others, it is not self-seeking, it is not easily angered, it keeps no record of wrongs."

4th: "Love does not boast" The Greek word *phusioutai* translated into boasts means "to act or play the braggart." It's a word that describes an ostentatious attitude. It's the same word that was used in the New Testament to refer to academic or intellectual pride. I had a Seminary Professor who once said, "It takes twenty years to get an education and another twenty years to get over it." His point was, the higher you get on the ladder of education, if you don't watch it, the more your tendency will be to look down on those who haven't climbed with you, and if you're not careful you'll become arrogant. And that attitude will continue until you discover that you're really just a chihuahua in the midst of Saint Bernards. And then you'll discover that you're really not all that you thought you were.

If you compare yourself with others, you will always find someone far more superior. And so you'll climb harder and harder, but eventually you'll run into another Saint Bernard and it will be one frustrating experience after another. Why can't we just be what we are? We're basically just gobs of mud with a few dust bunnies mixed in. And by God's grace, we're provided with a heart that beats 110,000 times a day, lungs that pump oxygen, a mouth that speaks and emotions that can love. What do we have to boast about? Love does not boast.

5th: "Love is not proud." By the way, boasting is what we do;

proud is what we are. The word proud means, "to blow." Have you ever been around someone who constantly talks about his or her accomplishments, and no matter what you say, they have a bigger and better story or example? They're constantly dropping names of important people they know. We sometimes describe a person like that as a "big blow hard." In other words, they're arrogant; they're prideful. They'll disguise it by constantly commenting on how humble they are. Don't be fooled; false humility comes from a place of pride. That's this word that Paul uses here.

By the way, churches can also become proud and arrogant. Paul writes in 1 Corinthians 4:6-7: "Now, brothers and sisters, I have applied these things to myself and Apollos for your benefit, so that you may learn from us the meaning of the saying, 'Do not go beyond what is written.' Then you will not be puffed up in being a follower of one of us over against the other. For who makes you different from anyone else? What do you have that you did not receive? And if you did receive it, why do you boast as though you did not?"

That's just simple, plain logic. Paul says, "Here you are thinking that you're really impressive; but everything you are, you've received. And if you've received it, why are you taking the credit for it? You didn't earn it; it was given to you." And so when Paul says, "Love does not boast and is not proud," that's what he's talking about.

If you really want to have a ministry with other people, and I think most of us do, there must be the removal of false arrogance and pride that builds itself up around us. There has to be that willingness to accept one who hasn't achieved all that we have. Love is not proud.

6th: "Love does not dishonor others." At the heart of the word dishonor is the Greek, word *scama*. The word means scheme. It's the idea of a shape or a form that's outward. You can see the *scama* of this book. It has a certain shape; it has an outward appearance. Sometimes this word is translated as un-becoming. In other words, love is not, on the outward appear-ance, unbecoming. I think the best substitute from our English lexicon would be tactless — love is not tactless. By the way, con-servative, legalistic Christianity has turned out a lot of countless tactless, rude, sharp, blunt Christians. And those kinds of Chris-tians are easy to spot because they always look unhappy and miserable. It's as if they were born on the dark side of the moon, weaned on pickle juice, and baptized in vinegar! And there's nothing wrong with being a conservative Christian; just don't act like it and do your best not to look like it. Don't get me wrong, we should be conservative in our belief of what God has said in His Word, but our love must be tactful. Otherwise, we're turning people off. Paul tells us that love says the proper thing, at the proper time, in the loving way.

I think that most of us mean well when we are dealing with the people that God has placed in our lives, but often we fail to put ourselves in the other person's place. As Christians, we sometimes convey the idea that it doesn't matter if we offend people and we justify it by claiming to be "defenders of truth and righteousness!" Paul says, "Love doesn't act like that. It doesn't dishonor others, it's not rude and tactless." This may be the number one reasons our neighbors don't understand the gospel. Ask your neighbor to give you some words that come to mind when they think of Christians. You will hear words like rude, narrow, obnoxious, pious, abrasive, judgmental, and ar-gumentative, but you probably won't hear the words kind and loving and tactful and empathetic. And maybe that explains why our neighbors don't know about the hope that's found in a rela-tionship with God. It's because we often come across as unbe-coming. They haven't seen this kind of love in our lives. Love does not dishonor others.

7th: "Love is not self-seeking." Do you know what it literally says in the original Greek language? It says, "love does not seek the things of itself." In other words, agape doesn't seek its own interests and rights. It isn't selfish; it doesn't always have to be first.

We never outgrow our childish ways, do we? We always want to be first. I was at Target one day during the Christmas holidays and it was crowded and there were two ladies in front of me jockeying for the next place in line. I finally asked, "Would you guys like me to referee?" They gave me a not-very-nice look. And we all have days like that; we're human. But if I had a dollar for every person that has told me that they walked away from church because they were treated rudely, I'd be a rich man...and often it was by someone on the church staff! It breaks my heart every time I hear a story like that. But at the end of the day, what goes on inside the walls of our churches is one thing, but if our love isn't coming through to those outside of the walls of our churches, according to Paul, it's worth nothing — zero. Everything we do is in vain.

Will you allow me to make this practical? How you shop reveals rather you have this kind of love or not. How you treat people in the service industry reveals rather you have this kind of love or not. How you talk to your wife or husband, or children, or neighbor, or coworker reveals whether you've got it or not. How you relate to the person that's abrasive reveals if you have it or not. That's where it's at; that's where the rubber meets the road. Love is not self-seeking.

8th: "Love is not provoked." The word provoked comes from two Greek words that mean, sharpen and alongside. And if you're like me, you probably wonder how this idea grew out of those words. Well, the negative says, "love is not sharpened alongside." In other words, when someone is standing alongside a person who is sharp and bitter and irritating, the one with real love doesn't pick up that sharpness and irritation. Another way of saying it would be, "real love doesn't draw to itself the sharp characteristics of others."

There's an old saying, "We become like the ones we spend our time with." But agape love is unaffected when it's alongside those who are sharp and irritating. 1 Peter 4:8 says: "Above all, love each other deeply, because love covers over a multitude of sins." See the word deeply? It's an athletic term used to describe a runner when he's stretching his muscles to the max as he reaches for the finish line. It's the idea of maximum, intense effort toward reaching the goal. In other words, love is not provoked because it works at maximum effort not to be provoked. That means that when you love this way, you are able to see beyond a person's sin or failure, and instead of writing that person off, you can love that person. And that leads right into the next characteristic of agape love.

9th: "Love keeps no record of wrongs." This is an accountant's term. It's a reference to placing something into a ledger for a permanent record. But in this case, it's not a business term; it's a term for the mind. Paul is saying, "When you really love this way, you don't place the wrongs done against you into the ledger of your permanent memory." Another way of saying it would be, "When you love this way, you don't sit around and sulk and pout when people take advantage of you." This kind of love doesn't allow our minds to become a depository for unexpressed resentment.

I once read the story of John Wesley, a 16th-century British Theologian, as he was making a voyage with a friend named General Oglethorpe. On the journey, Wesley witnessed Oglethorpe rebuking and threatening a servant with revenge because of something the servant had done. Afterwards, Wesley confronted Oglethorpe and encouraged him to overlook the offense and to let it go, Oglethorpe looked at Wesley and said, "I never forgive and I never forget." Wesley responded, "Well sir, then I hope you never sin." I speak from experience; you have to sin and fail and be rejected before you can realize the importance of a love that doesn't hold a grudge.

I'll address this topic in detail later in another chapter, but let me ask you a question, and be honest. Are you carrying around a grudge? I was talking to a young lady recently about a situation in her life where someone had hurt her and she told me, "I'm really good any holding a grudge." Does that describe you? Are you holding onto resentment against another person because of something they did to you or said about you? Real love has the marvelous ability not to record that; it's able to flush it right out of the mind.

Take this seriously. Jesus made it very clear that if you carry around resentment, God will see to it that you are tortured until there's forgiveness. And I know that those are strong words, but until you forgive, you'll never find relief and peace. But even worse, you'll never know real love. "Love keeps no record of wrongs."

10th: "Love does not delight in evil." Paul is saying, "Love has no sympathy in wrongdoing; it finds zero pleasure in it." Ephesians 5 tells us that when we sin, the Holy Spirit is grieved. We literally hurt the Holy Spirit's feelings! It's the same way with real love. Real love has its heart broken when the object of that love is unrighteous. "Love does not delight in evil."

11th: "Love rejoices with the truth." There's a partnership here with the previous characteristic; love and truth are partners; they're to be seen as twins, and you can't really have one without the other. The person that you genuinely love is one that you feel free to be open and honest with. But if you don't really love someone you'll say things like, "I'm not going to tell them how I really feel because I don't want to hurt them." That isn't love. Genuine love basks in the sunlight of the truth.

The people who have been my closest friends over the years are the people who have leveled with me in the area of truth. In fact, I'm so glad that I have an individual who does that for me now, whether I want to hear it or not. Solomon writes in Proverbs 27:6: "Wounds from a friend can be trusted, but an enemy multiplies kisses." Literally it says, "Trustworthy are the bruises caused by a wounding of one who loves you." You can be thankful when someone loves you so much that they'll tell you the truth. Love rejoices with the truth.

12th: "Love always protects," This word, protect was used in the first-century to describe a warrior who covered himself with his shield to protect himself from darts and the arrows. I think what Paul is saying is that real love withstands the blows of others. It doesn't get sidetracked because others take shots at you. I want to make this personal so I came up with a test of three questions to help you see how you're doing in this area.

First, let's say you've done something very nice for a friend. Maybe it cost you your time; maybe it cost you financially; maybe it cost you both. The friend you performed this act of kindness or generosity for doesn't seem grateful. Are you hurt? If your love always protects, you don't allow it to offend you. You don't need a thank you note. You don't need an expression of gratitude for the love to continue.

Second, you share something in confidence with someone you love and later on you discover that what you shared was shared by that person with someone else. Does that ruin your friendship? I'm not saying what the person did was right; I'm saying that it shouldn't destroy the relationship. By the way, as we saw earlier, our relationships are too often built on conditions. And if those conditions fail, that's often the end of the relationship. Real love that protects works through those times.

Third, you have a friend who is sick and they really need you, and so you go out of your way to help them. You take them meals. You drive them to their doctor's appointment. You go to the pharmacy and pick up his or her prescriptions. Sometime later you fall ill and your friend doesn't even call to check on you. Are you hurt? Love always protects.

13th: "Love always trusts." Of the entire list of the fifteen characteristics of love, this one bothered me the most. It sounds

like love is gullible and undiscerning. But the Greek word translated *trust* here means unsuspicious. Literally it says, "Love isn't
suspicious." Instead, this kind of love is trusting; it gives the benefit of the doubt; it's not cynical.

When I was in college, I worked at a grocery store. Several
of us would go into work at night after the store closed and we
would through the night restocking the shelves and getting
everything ready for the following day. What I remember the
most about that job is that we had the most suspicious man as a
boss that I've ever met in my life. He was suspicious of everything and everyone. He was constantly watching to make sure
no one took a day-old muffin from the bakery. He made sure
that no one took more than the allotted time for a break. He
would actually hide behind displays and watch us work to make
sure we weren't slacking off. Does that describe you? Are you
that way with your employees? Are you that way with your
kids? Are you that way with your spouse? If so, you're moving
quickly towards marriage on the rocks. Nothing will destroy
love quicker than jealousy; it's as severe as the grave. Love always trusts.

14th and 15th: Love always hopes and perseveres. A godly
man by the name of Lenny Moen was the closest thing I ever
had to a mentor. He said to me when I was just starting out in
the ministry as a wise twenty-four year old, "Mike, to follow this
calling, you must have an incurable confidence in God's ability
to change people's lives." That's what Paul is saying here. When
you really love, you don't give up on people. There's an incurable confidence that God is at work. Love always hopes and perseveres.

Now what do we do with this kind of instruction? There are
several possible responses you could have. One response would
be, "Starting today, I'm never going to be unlovely again. From
this moment on, I'm never going to share anything but love."
Well, as noble as that sounds, that's the wrong response! It's also

an unrealistic response that will last about as long as it takes you to read this chapter. If you're really good, I'll give you until sundown, but it won't last long because, in your own strength, you will fail.

A second response could be, "I've tried to love this way but I've failed so it isn't worth the effort or the risk." But Romans 12:10 says, "Be devoted to one another in love." And so it would be disobedient to say, "I'm not even going to try."

But there's a third possible response, and this is the proper one: "I admire these qualities and I want them, but I can't produce them. So, God, I'm willing to change in each of these areas, but you will have to do it through me." And when you give God that kind of ammunition, He can fire away and never run out of shells. In fact, it's amazing how all God really wants is a willing spirit. He wants to be in control. And it may be awkward at first, but if we will begin to act in agape love toward others, regardless of our emotions or the awkwardness we may feel, soon we will discover that our actions have changed our feelings. For example, do you feel that someone is a little strange? Show him a little agape; your disapproval will soon turn into acceptance. Is someone irritating you? Show them a little agape; your anger will grow into patience. Believe me, it takes courage. It takes courage to act better than you feel. It takes courage to give better than you receive, but we've seen this courage before. It's cross courage; it's Gethsemane grit. And because Jesus chose to build his life on this kind of love, we who were nothing have the opportunity to be sons and daughters of God. People all around you are waiting for a similar love to transform their lives in a similar way.

That's the list, and it's overwhelming, isn't it? And I know what some of you are thinking. You're thinking, "If I love this way, I'm going to be vulnerable; people will take advantage of me and run over me." You're not wrong. At some point in your life, you're going to get out on a relational limb and somebody's going to saw it off. And as you tumble down you're going to ask, "Was it worth it?"

In his book, The Four Loves, C.S. Lewis says it this way: "To love at all is to be vulnerable. Love anything and your heart will be rung and possibly broken. If you want to make sure of keeping your heart in tact, you must give you heart to no one, not even an animal. Wrap it around carefully with hobbies and little luxuries. Avoid all entanglements. Lock it up safely in the casket or coffin of your selfishness. And in that casket, safe, dark, motionless, airless, it will change — it will not be broken. It will become unbreakable, irredeemable...the only place outside Heaven where you can be perfectly safe from all the dangers of love is in Hell."

Those are your options. Are you willing to take the risk? The ball is in your court.

Chapter 6

"You Have to Take the Good With the Bad!"

When the news of my moral failure became public, as you can imagine, my world was immediately turned upside down. My family was wrecked. Forty years of ministry was instantly destroyed. My reputation and character were shattered. I was suddenly unemployed. My financial security was history. My retirement plan vanished. My friends disappeared. Some of my family members turned their backs on me. I felt like an outcast, a leper. I was unclean. It was an incredibly stressful time. With thousands of people in the community knowing everything about everything I did, there was no rock that I could hide under. Everywhere I went, I ran into someone that reminded me of my failure. I'll never forget the evening I was at a restaurant, and I walked by a table where a couple from my church was sitting with an older couple. I said hello to the younger couple and the wife said to the older couple with great fanfare, "Mom and Dad, this is the pastor who committed adultery and destroyed our church." That comment caught the attention of several surrounding tables that had no idea that dinner also included a show. It was an incredibly awkward moment, but I was guilty as charged. It was during that period that God graciously brought a few men into my life who came alongside me to love and support me though this time. They informed me that they weren't there to judge me, confront me, or even fix me. They were there because they loved and accepted me unconditionally. They committed themselves to help me carry the burden that was of my own making.

But if you're been around church for a while, it won't surprise you that these men were criticized by some for accepting me where I was without judging me. I was told that I only surrounded myself with people who told me what I wanted to hear. But these men never approved of my behavior, in fact the exact opposite is true, yet they did accept me as a person. The tension arises from the fact that in the perspective of some Christians acceptance equals approval. It was those men that God used greatly to get me through my nightmare. They provided a safe haven and a refuge in the midst of my storm, but it was only possible because of their acceptance of me as a person instead of their rejection of me because of my actions. It didn't fix everything, but it taught me some valuable lessons. Trust me, there's a different perspective when you find yourself on the other side of the fence. So, in this chapter I want to talk about the sheer power of biblical acceptance in each of our lives when it comes to the process of restoring a life.

I want to begin with a little theological lesson. The New Testament consists of a bunch of letters that guys, like Peter, James and Paul, who wrote to some churches that had been established in the first century. And these letters essentially did two things: First, they taught what to believe. Second, they explained how to love one another. Do you know why the writers focused on those two topics? It's because the main challenge for people in the first century was the same challenge that we all face today: people just couldn't get along. These letters taught a lot about what it takes to keep relationships healthy. As a result, these guys spent a lot of time describing what it looks like to love each other. And if you take the time to do the research, you'll discover that there are twenty-six "one anothers" in the New Testament, and those twenty-six "one anothers" basically focus on four keys to loving one another: We have to accept one another, we have to forgive one another, we have to submit to one another, and we have to care for one another. And let's be honest, that's a lot easier to say than to actually do, and so I want to talk about what this would look like in our relationships. More importantly, it's going to give us some insight as to how to love and restore the broken lives that we come in contact with every day.

I want to begin by addressing the area that I believe may be the toughest of the four for Christians to wrap their heads around, but, more importantly, it's the key to being able to pull off the other three: We have to accept one another. And I'll go ahead and let you know what a big part of the problem is. Often when we use the word accept, what we really mean is tolerate. In other words, "I'm going to tolerate you the way you are. I'm not going to try to change you, but I'm not going to hang out with you or like you either." And so, in our relationships, we're really just tolerating each other, but we use the word accept.

So, what does it mean to accept one another? Let me give you a definition that will help: Acceptance is the ability to receive another person without internal restrictions or external requirements. The internal restrictions have to do with our prejudices. Let's be honest, we all have areas inside of us that bristle when we meet certain people. Maybe they don't look the way you look. Maybe they vote Republican, and you vote Democrat. Maybe they've been blessed financially and you struggle from paycheck to paycheck. Maybe their kids go to a private school but your kids go to public school. Maybe they wore a mask during COVID and you refused too. Too soon? My point is, we all have prejudices that prevent us from accepting certain people into our lives. Those prejudices fall into the category of internal restrictions.

But then there are also the external requirements, and these outer requirements have to do with performance. Maybe you reared your child to live a certain way but now he or she isn't living the way you brought them up. Maybe they have a different sexual orientation and that makes you bristle inside. Maybe you have a lofty degree or multiple degrees, but your child is perfectly satisfied with a high school diploma or GED and that difference of opinion affects the relationship. Whether we want to admit it or not, all of us have people in our lives that don't measure up to our expectations. And our typical reaction is to push those individuals out of our lives until we're ready to let them back in, which usually means, "When they get their act together and do what I think they should do."

But biblical acceptance means that an individual is valuable just as they are…and this is where we get hung up. Most Christians feel that if they accept someone, they are approving of their behavior. But acceptance doesn't mean approval. It means that you accept that person as they are. It means that you have room in your life for that person regardless of their actions or behavior.

This is where the tension comes: As Christians, we have been invited into a relationship with God, and that relationship is characterized by unconditional love and unconditional acceptance, both of which are rare in this world. But once we accept the invitation of being in a relationship with God through the power of the gospel, we are commanded to treat the people in our lives the way that God has treated us. In other words, God says, "All of this great stuff you have going on with me, I want you to now extend to the people I've put in your life. And just as you've been unconditionally forgiven, I want you to unconditionally forgive. And I don't want you to forgive because you think they deserve to be forgiven, I want you to forgive because I've forgiven you. And I also want you to accept them, love them and be merciful to them. And I don't want you to respond to them the way they deserve to be responded to. I want you to respond to them the way I've responded to you." And that sounds so great on the surface, but let's be honest, that's tough, isn't it?

By the way, I want you to know ahead of time that I will not answer all of your questions about acceptance in this chapter. My goal is simply to give you a different perspective through which to view the people in your life who are unacceptable to you. Maybe they're not acceptable because of your prejudices. Maybe they're not acceptable because they haven't performed up to your expectations. I want to give you a brand new lens to look through. And if you'll begin viewing people through this lens, you'll figure out what to do in your relationships no matter how complicated the situation is.

By the way, God designed each of us to be acceptance magnets. This explains why teenagers take the advice of their peers over the advice of their parents. It's not that their peers are smarter or that they have more life experience. It's just that we're far more open to the influence of those who accept us than we are to those who lecture us. Even though all of us want to be accepted, we all have people in our lives that we refuse to accept. But then we become Christians and God says to us, "I want you to learn to accept others the way I've accepted you," which means we have to break the habit of only accepting acceptable people. It means that we have to break the habit of only accepting people that meet our expectations. It means that when we're wounded deeply by people we love and everything inside of us wants to say, "When you get your act together, I'll consider letting you back into my life," our Heavenly Father says, "You've got to break that habit because I'm calling you to a whole, new standard."

Let me show you how Paul put it in Romans 15:5-6: "May the God who gives endurance and encouragement give you the same attitude of mind toward each other that Christ Jesus had, so that with one mind and one voice you may glorify the God and Father of our Lord Jesus Christ." This is what Paul is saying in this letter to the Christians in Rome: "I know that you guys come from all different walks of life. Some of you are young and some of you are old. Some of you are slaves and some of you are free. Some of you are Jews and some of you are Gentiles. Some of you are rich and some of you are poor. But you're all following Jesus, so you should all be going in the same general direction. And as a result, there ought to be incredible unity among you."

And then Paul goes on to say in Romans 15:7: "Accept one another, then..." By the way, when you accept someone, it's like catching a football. You reach out and receive it and then you bring it to yourself. That's a picture of what it looks like to accept someone. And Paul says, "As Christians, we should be in the habit of reaching out and receiving other people, and then bringing them into our lives." And then he tells us what that should look like in the next part of Romans 15:7: "Accept one another, then, just as Christ accepted you." And let's be honest, that's a pretty high standard because many of us would have to admit that when we became Christians, we weren't very acceptable, but God didn't ask us to change anything. He just went ahead and accepted us; He reached out and received us, and then we started making changes. That means that if we're going to accept other people the way that God has accepted us, then we have to get into the habit of accepting people where they are before they change. That also means that we have to accept them where they are before they become acceptable.

And look at how Paul concludes Romans 15:7: "Accept one another, then, just as Christ accepted you, in order to bring praise to God." Do you know why that brings praise to God? Think about it this way: When we praise someone, it's because they went beyond the norm. For example we don't praise people for just doing the basic run-of-the mill things (unless it involves kid's sports, and then every kid gets a trophy). No wife says, "Way to go honey; you watched the entire football game." No parent says to their child, "Oh honey, I'm so proud of you; you finished all your ice cream." We don't praise people for doing the norm. We praise people when they go above and beyond. We praise an individual when they go the extra mile.

Paul says that it's a really big deal that God accepted you the way you were because you weren't very acceptable. And it's also a really big deal when we accept people who have disappointed us and hurt us and haven't acted acceptable. Everybody gets extra credit because that's not the cultural norm The cultural norm is this: "As soon as you get your act together I'll consider receiving you into my life relationally, but until then, you're out." But God would respond, "Let's rethink that! I got big-time extra credit and praise when I sent my Son to die for unacceptable people, and now I want you to do for others, what I've done for you."

But here's where it gets complicated and difficult because, as Christians, to respond that way to others would require us to stop trying to be right about everything. We have to stop having the goal of winning arguments, and having been around church all of my life, I know how hard that is for Christians to do. And so, for acceptance to become a lifestyle, it means that some things in us are going to have to change. In fact, this is what's really interesting about Jesus. Jesus didn't come into the world to be right. Jesus didn't come into the world to make a point; that wasn't His purpose. If Jesus would have come into the world just to be right, He would have gone around saying, "You're wrong; you're wrong; you're wrong; you're wrong! Wrong action, wrong thought, wrong attitude, wrong motive; everything in your life is wrong! Now, follow me." Let me ask you a question; do you think such an approach to a lost humanity would have been effective? The answer is, "Absolutely not!" Nobody would have followed Jesus if His reason for being here was just to be right about everything. He was holy and perfect and pure; He was the Son of God. He knew all the answers; He knew every man and woman's heart. He could have just lined people up and told them how wrong they were, but Jesus rarely did that. He walked and lived among wrong, sinful people, but His reason for being on this earth wasn't just to expose how wrong and sinful everybody was. Do you know why He was here? It was to build a bridge and to win our affection. He was here to accept unacceptable people. And now He says to you and me, "I want you to do that. Your goal isn't to win an argument; your goal is to win their heart. Your goal isn't to be right or make a point; your goal is to build a bridge. I didn't call you to convince anybody of anything; I called you to accept them." And when that becomes the new lens through which we view our relationships, it has the power to transform our relationships, just as God, through that same lens, has transformed many of our lives.

But here's the problem with most Christians: we want both; we want to win their hearts and we want to win the argument. We want to make a point and we want to build a bridge. We want to convince them and we want to accept them. Well, I've got great news: both are possible because that's exactly what God did. But here's where we have to begin to think differently, because here is where the power is. If you want to accomplish both, then you have to focus on building a bridge, not making a point. You have to focus on accepting, not convincing. You have to focus on winning a heart, not an argument. And when that becomes the focus, then you'll attain influence. And maybe, by God's grace, He'll use you to change the person that you're so convinced needs changing. But it all begins with accepting, because that's what God did for you and me.

During my forty years of ministry, I often found myself involved in counseling situations. I remember one couple in particular. The husband had blown it big time. And after explaining the situation and the conflict, the wife concluded her thoughts by saying to me, "Tell him I'm right! I've already shown him the verses; just tell him I'm right!" To which I responded, "You've already told him that you're right and if I tell him that you're right, is that really going to fix everything? Are you guys going to walk out of here best friends if I tell him you're right?" And she responded, "I don't know; I haven't thought about it that far. I just want him to realize that I'm right." And that may sound like the kind of conversation that takes place around your house. But this is what you need to know when you find yourself in a situation like that: while you were still a sinner, your Heavenly Father decided to win your heart, not make a point. He didn't try to convince you; He didn't try to build a case, He decided to build a bridge. And if He did that for us, shouldn't we do that for the people that He's put in our lives? I'm not saying that it's easy. There are no predictable outcomes, and sometimes it's even messy. You'll watch the people you love the most make the most horrible decisions imaginable. But if you will decide to build a bridge, and if you will choose to accept instead of convince, then you'll attain influence. And there are no guarantees, but perhaps God will use that influence to move that individual in His direction. But I promise you this: you will never influence anyone who doesn't feel accepted by you.

Over the past forty years, I've seen it all; I've counseled in every situation imaginable. I've talked with parents after they discovered that a son or daughter was gay, and they wanted to cut all ties with them. I've talked with young men and women that are gay and they decided they didn't want to have a relationship with their parents anymore. I've talked with pregnant girls that weren't married and the parents that wanted to disown them. I've talked with prodigals and addicts and I've talked with the friends and family that are being affected by their behavior, and the relationships are always broken down. And everybody that finds themselves in one of those situations thinks they're right. This is what I tell them: In those moments, that's not even the issue. The issue is, "How do I do for this person, who at this moment seems unacceptable, what God did for me when I was equally unacceptable?" The question is, "How do I build a bridge; how do I win a heart? How do I accept, not, how do I convince?" And if that becomes the new lens, through which we view individuals, then we are simply imitating our Heavenly Father.

And when we do that, we invite God in on the outcome of

the situation, because we have become for other people what God has so graciously been for us. For some of you, this isn't all that hard. For some of you, it's excruciatingly difficult. For all of us, there's someone in our life that has the potential to break our heart and deeply disappoint us. And as a result, our tendency is to respond in kind instead of saying, "God, this is my opportunity to give you praise because I'm going to do for that person what you so graciously did for me."

I'll be honest with you, the inability of most Christians to grasp this principle is why so many of our churches are empty. It's why so many have walked away with no intention of ever returning.

You can see the value of living this way in probably the most well-known story in the Bible; it's the story of the prodigal son. It's the story of a young man who asked his father for his inheritance so he could take off and do his own thing. And he headed off to the big city where he partied his brains out until one day he went to the ATM to make a withdrawal and the screen read, "Insufficient funds." And if you're familiar with the story, you know that eventually he found himself feeding pigs and scavenging around to eat whatever was left over after the pigs finished their meal. And in that pigpen, maybe leaning up against a fencepost he thought, "How did I ever end up here?"

And Luke 15:17-25 says: "When he came to his senses, he said, 'How many of my father's hired servants have food to spare, and here I am starving to death! I will set out and go back to my father and say to him: Father, I have sinned against heaven and against you. I am no longer worthy to be called your son; make me like one of your hired servants.' So, he got up and went to his father. But while he was still a long way off, his father saw him and was filled with compassion for him; he ran to his son, threw his arms around him and kissed him. The son said to him, 'Father, I have sinned against heaven and against you. I am no longer worthy to be called your son.' But the father said to his servants, 'Quick! Bring the best robe and put it on him. Put a ring on his finger. Bring the fattened calf and kill it. Let's have a feast and celebrate. For this son of mine was dead and is alive again; he was lost and is found. So, they began to celebrate. Meanwhile, the older son was in the field. When he came near the house, he heard music and dancing."

Then he sees a servant and asks, "Hey, what's the hoopla all about?" And the servant says, "Haven't you heard, Bubba's back, and your dad killed that calf we've been fattening up and he's throwing the social event of the year." And when the older brother heard the news that Bubba was back, he responded, "Oh, thank God; I'm so relieved!" No, that wasn't his response at all. He was angry; he was livid; he was ticked off. So, he goes up to his room to pout and when the father hears about it, he takes the napkin off his chin and excuses himself from the table and he goes and finds his oldest son so he can encourage him to join in the celebration.

But notice the older brother's response in Luke 15:29-30: "All these years I've been slaving for you and never disobeyed your orders. Yet you never gave me even a young goat so I could celebrate with my friends. But when this son of yours who has squandered your property with prostitutes comes home, you kill the fattened calf for him." This is the Older Brother Syndrome. It's when we look down on others and refuse to accept them because, from our perspective, they're not as good as we are. It's when we see ourselves as better than others. In fact, let me give you some symptoms of the Older Brother Syndrome.

Symptom #1: You'd rather judge people than accept people.

Symptom #2: You're disappointed when people don't get what you think they deserve.

Symptom #3: You're angry when it appears that God blesses others regardless of their bad behavior

Symptom #4: You often say things like, "I would never do that," even though, deep down inside you'd like to!

That's the Older Brother Syndrome; that's self-righteousness, and it affects how we see others and it short-circuits our ability to accept them. But not only that, it affects the way we see ourselves because we see ourselves as being better than others.

It reminds me of a story in Luke 7:36-43, 47: "When one of the Pharisees invited Jesus to have dinner with him, he went to the Pharisee's house and reclined at the table. A woman in that town who lived a sinful life learned that Jesus was eating at the Pharisee's house, so she came there with an alabaster jar of perfume. As she stood behind him at his feet weeping, she began to wet his feet with her tears. Then she wiped them with her hair, kissed them and poured perfume on them. When the Pharisee who had invited him saw this, he said to himself, 'If this man were a prophet, he would know who is touching him and what kind of woman she is — that she is a sinner.' Jesus answered him, 'Simon, I have something to tell you.' 'Tell me, teacher,' he said. 'Two people owed money to a certain moneylender. One owed him five hundred denarii, and the other fifty. Neither of them had the money to pay him back, so he forgave the debts of both. Now which of them will love him more?' Simon replied, 'I suppose the one who had the bigger debt forgiven.' 'You have judged correctly,' Jesus said...'Therefore, I tell you, her many sins have been forgiven — as her great love has shown. But whoever has been forgiven little loves little.'"

One of the reasons I love this story so much is because it doesn't teach what we think it teaches, in fact, it teaches the opposite. We think the story gives credibility to the fact that there are some people who are really bad sinners and they've been forgiven a lot, and since they've been forgiven a lot, out of appreciation, they love God a lot, and that makes sense. And then there are some people who aren't that bad and so they only need to be forgiven a little bit. And since they're not as appreciative because they haven't been forgiven for a lot, they only love Jesus a little bit. Here's the problem with that logic: There are a lot of people, many of you included, that are much better than I'll ever be. Some of you are darn near saints! And since that's the case, that means that you can't love Jesus as much as I can because you haven't had to be forgiven for as much as I have. And so for you to love a lot, you've got to get busy and do a lot of really bad stuff so you can be forgiven of a lot and then you can love a lot. You need to have an affair and smoke cigars and eat gummies and drink lots of bourbon and bet on the horses and kick the neighbor's dog, and then you can be forgiven for a lot and, as a result, you will be so thankful. But is that what Jesus meant? Well you have to remember that Jesus was addressing Simon's thoughts, and Simon was thinking, "I only owe God a little bit because I'm not that bad of a sinner, but because she's a really bad sinner, she owes a lot." This is the problem with that kind of thinking: If you don't think you're as bad as others, you're not going to be as grateful as others, and so Jesus is teaching that there are some people who think they're better than others. From their perspective, their past isn't as bad; they haven't sinned as much, but that's faulty thinking. James 2:10 says: "For whoever keeps the whole law and yet stumbles at just one point (from God's perspective) is guilty of breaking all of it."

But when you're self-righteous, you don't see that. The Older Brother Syndrome affects how we see others but it also affects how we see the Father. And it's because, if you suffer from the Older Brother Syndrome, you're so focused on how good you are and how bad everyone else is, you miss out on how good God is to you. That's why the older brother said in Luke 15:29: "All these years I've been slaving for you and never disobeyed your orders. Yet you never gave me even a young goat so I could celebrate with my friends." By the way, that's not true and I'll show you why. It says in Luke 15:11-12: "Jesus continued: There was a man who had two sons. The younger one said to his Father, "Father, give me my share of the estate. So, he divided his property between them. "You see, when we read the story, we assume that when the younger son asked for his inheritance, the father gave it to him, and that's it. But the father also gave the older son his inheritance at the same time he gave it to the younger son. And if you're familiar with Jewish tradition, you know that the older son, the firstborn, always got twice as much. But that's how self-righteousness thinks. It says, "You weren't fair to me." The father should have said, "You're right, I wasn't fair. I gave you twice as much even though you didn't deserve it." But notice the father's response to the son's comment, "You never even gave me a young goat so I could party with my friends." Luke 15:31: "My son," the father said, "you are always with me, and everything I have is yours." "You are always with me…" (that represents the presence of God), "and everything I have is yours…" (that represents the provision of God).

And this is what is really sad about this story. The younger son missed out on the presence and provision of the Father because he left home. And the older son missed out on the presence and provision of the Father because his heart left home. He may have never left physically, but his heart did.

So, how do we avoid the Older Brother Syndrome so we can be accepting of others the way God has accepted us? I can tell you that the answer isn't just to study the Bible. That may be a part of the answer but not all the answer. In fact, Paul tells us 1 Corinthians 8:1 that knowledge alone puffs up; It makes us arrogant and unaccepting. It makes us like the older brother. But knowledge isn't the problem. Paul never criticizes knowledge, in fact, he encourages us to grow in our faith by becoming knowledgeable of God's Word. Paul is just saying what we already know; knowledge alone makes us arrogant. And we all know knowledgeable, arrogant Christians, and if you're like me, you avoid them like the plague. But knowledge doesn't have to make us arrogant. Growing up spiritually doesn't have to make us obnoxious. In fact, this is coming from a guy who wrote thirteen of the twenty-seven books that make up the NT, which is thirteen more than any of us wrote! So, Paul is like the Big Kahuna of apostles; it's safe to say he grew up. But did he develop Older Brother Syndrome?

Let me show you something that maybe you've never seen before. The first book that Paul wrote was the book of Galatians (AD 53). This is how he began the book in Galatians 1:1: "Paul, an apostle…" In other words, "I just want you to know, I'm a big deal." Three years later he wrote in 1 Corinthians 15:9: "For I am the least of the apostles and do not even deserve to be called an apostle." By the way, Paul became a Christian in AD 36, and he wrote this in AD 56. That means that Paul had been a believer for twenty years. And after twenty years Paul writes, "I'm not worthy to be called an apostle. In fact, I'm the least of the apostles." In AD 63 (7 years later), Paul writes this in Ephesians 3:8: "I am less than the least of all God's people." Paul began by saying: "I'm the least of the apostles." Seven years later he writes, "I've re-evaluated this whole thing. Actually, I'm less than the least of all of God's people." Two years later (AD 65) which is one year before Paul's death, Paul writes this in 1 Timothy 1:15: "Christ Jesus came into the world to save sinners – of whom I am the worst." Let me show you why Paul never developed the Older Brother Syndrome. 1 Corinthians 2:2 (NLT): "For I decided to concentrate only on Jesus Christ and his death on the cross."

Make no mistake about it, in the story of the prodigal son, there were two rebels under one roof. In the same way, there are two kinds of rebels under every church roof, we just carry out our rebellion in different ways. There are some rebels that we consider detestable, shameless, and unacceptable. And then there are others that are deceitful, self-righteous, and proud, but both require grace in dealing with them. Do you know what breaks my heart? It breaks my heart to realize that there are millions of prodigals still living out there in the pigpen in some distant land, and they're miserable. And one of the main reasons they're out there and not inside of our churches is because of the

Older Brother Syndrome. And I believe that a lot of those broken, hurting, lonely prodigals who would love to come home to the father. They miss the father; they love the father, they just don't like us very much.

Do you suffer from Older Brother Syndrome? Is it hard for you to accept people without internal restrictions or external requirements? If it is, you have the disease. But what if we all decided to work really hard at extending our arms to the wounded, broken, hurting, lonely, disenfranchised people around us. What if all of the people that make up our congregations and small groups had the attitude, "We don't care where you've been or what you've done, we're just glad you're back; I accept you where you are and we'll go forward from here."

Let me close this chapter by asking you a personal question. If a prodigal returned home from the pigpen today and you were the first person that met them, would they feel welcomed home? Would they feel accepted unconditionally? Would they stay or would they feel rejected and turn around and leave again? Aren't you glad that our Heavenly Father doesn't beat us down for how wrong we are? Aren't you grateful for His grace and mercy? He says, "As I have accepted you, you accept one another." Easy to say, but hard to do. But everything we're going to talk about from here on out depends on the ability to imitate the Father in this area of our lives.

Chapter 7

"You Can't Fix Me, but You Can Sure Help!"

In AD 62, the Apostle Paul wrote a letter to a small church located in the city of Ephesus and that letter made its way into the Bible. We now know the letter as the Book of Ephesians. And Paul wrote in Ephesians 5:1-2: "Follow God's example, therefore, as dearly loved children and walk in the way of love, just as Christ loved us and gave himself up for us as a fragrant offering and sacrifice to God." And I read that and think, "Why is it so hard to imitate Jesus?" And I realize from a theological perspective that it goes back to our root problem called the Adamic Nature. That's a fancy theological term for the spiritual DNA that's been passed down to all of us from Adam and Eve's disobedience in the Garden of Eden. It's where we get the attitude that says, "I want to be right! I want my way! I want to be the boss!" But once we respond to the gospel and make the decision to follow Jesus, we suddenly find ourselves under the shadow of the cross of a man who came, not to be a boss, but a servant. And strangely, as we get to know Him, we realize that we want to be like Him. But it's then that we begin to experience the struggle between what we want in the flesh and what we know is better in the Spirit, and so the battle rages.

When you think of being a godly Christian, think of a cross because it will help you to remember the two dimensions. There is a vertical beam and a horizontal beam. The vertical beam represents our relationship with God. The horizontal beam represents our relationships with one another. When a Christian stands before God, two things should be true in our attitude as well as our actions. First, all power comes from God. That means that whatever God has allowed us to do, we openly admit that He gave us the power and the gifts and the energy to accomplish it. Second, all praise goes back to God. That makes sense doesn't it? He gives the power; He deserves the praise. That is the attitude that should pulsate through the veins of every Christian. And most Christians would agree with the position that God gets all the props whether we can actually live it out or not because there is a God, and we're not Him.

But when it comes to the horizontal, that's where it gets sticky. One man wrote, "To live above with saints we love, oh that will be glory; but to live below with the saints we know, well, that's a different story." He's just saying what we already know. Our problem isn't our vertical relationship with God; Jesus settled those battles. Our challenge is our horizontal relationships. Our greatest battles are with each other, especially when it comes to the matter of forgiveness. And what's interesting is that we all acknowledge that we are each in great need of forgiveness because we are all human. For example, at this very moment, some of you fall into the category of being the offended and you very much need to forgive the person who offended you so that they can experience forgiveness. Some of you fall into the category of being the offender and you very much need to be forgiven by the person you offended for doing the offending. Some of you may fall into both categories. My point is, it's a continual journey that we have to travel.

In 2 Corinthians 2, there's a real-life account of someone who needed to experience forgiveness. Paul writes in 2 Corinthians 2:4-6: "For I wrote you out of great distress and anguish of heart and with many tears, not to grieve you but to let you know the depth of my love for you. If anyone has caused grief, he has not so much grieved me as he has grieved all of you to some extent—not to put it too severely. The punishment inflicted on him by the majority is sufficient."

What is Paul talking about? What is he churning about on the inside? Well, there's a member in the church in Corinth who needs to be forgiven because he has paid sufficiently for what he has done. In fact, Paul adds in 2 Corinthians 2:7: "Now instead, you ought to forgive and comfort him, so that he will not be overwhelmed by excessive sorrow." By the way, Paul is referring to an issue that he wrote to this same church about about twelve months earlier. In 1 Corinthians 5, Paul addressed a sin that was public knowledge in the church at Corinth. He wrote in 1 Corinthians 5:1: "It is actually reported that there is sexual immorality among you, and of a kind that even pagans do not tolerate: A man is sleeping with his father's wife." And so there's a clear cut case of adult incest taking place in the church at Corinth; there's a man that's involved with his father's wife.

Paul continues in 1 Corinthians 5:2, 5: "And you are proud! Shouldn't you rather have gone into mourning and have put out of your fellowship the man who has been doing this? Hand this man over to Satan for the destruction of the flesh, so that his spirit may be saved on the day of the Lord." Those are strong words. I doubt you'll hear many sermons like that today. But this was public knowledge in this little church and the Corinthians were walking around bragging about what a grace-filled church they were. But Paul writes them and says, "That's not acceptable; don't allow it to continue! In fact, you need to disassociate yourself with this guy until he gets his act together."

And so I take it that over the next year they dealt with him severely, and apparently, over time, this guy confessed and repented and wanted back into the church, but they evidently kept beating this guy down. And so when Paul wrote the second letter to the church he said, "Back off; you've done your job. He doesn't need any more punishment; what he needs now is forgiveness." That's what 2 Corinthians 2 is all about. Paul is saying, "Enough is enough; let it go; forgive him."

In fact, I want you to see what Paul says about forgiveness in

2 Corinthians 2:10-11: "Anyone you forgive, I also forgive. And what I have forgiven—if there was anything to forgive—I have forgiven in the sight of Christ for your sake, in order that Satan might not outwit us. For we are not unaware of his schemes." I want you to notice that in this context of forgiveness, Paul brings in the work of Satan. And he says that if forgiveness is not adequately administered, you can open the door for Satan to go to work in your life. Do you understand the implications of that statement? If someone offends you and, because of your pride, you refuse to forgive them, you become open prey for the devil. And as a result, you can become the recipient of a harsher experience than the one going through the punishment. Instead of pride, what is really needed is humility and vulnerability.

In Matthew 5, Jesus says something about an aspect of vulnerability that is so rare, you seldom see it in action, but I believe that it can happen in our lives. I believe that we can be models of what this is all about. The verse is in Matthew 5:23: "Therefore, if you are offering your gift at the altar..." We don't present tithes and offerings at altars these days, so we need to understand the context of what Jesus is saying. Before we were given immediate access to God through Jesus' death, if you wanted to approach God, you had to bring two things; you had to bring an offering to be sacrificed and you needed a priest to represent your offering before God. Before Jesus' death, that's the way you found forgiveness and that's the way you found access to God. So, Jesus says in Matthew 5:23-24: "Therefore, if you are offering your gift at the altar and there remember that your brother or sister has something against you, leave your gift there in front of the altar. First go and be reconciled to them; then come and offer your gift." Notice that there is an order of events. You come to the altar with the offering, ready to worship God, and God puts on the brakes and says to you, "There's something between you and Frank; Frank is offended; go to Frank and make it right and then come back." And that sounds so simple to do, but being realistic, I want to address some "what if's."

"What if Frank refuses to forgive me?" The Greek word translated into the word reconciled in Matthew 5:24 means, "to alter or to change," and it has a little prefix attached to it that means, "to go through something." The literal meaning is, "through change." It's the idea of going through a process that brings about a change. But you go to the one you offended, and you discover that he doesn't want to forgive you. My guess is that we've all had that happen and it's devastating. Let me give you a verse that may help when you encounter a situation like that. Proverbs 16:7 says: "When the Lord takes pleasure in anyone's way, he causes their enemies to make peace with them." That's a great verse, but the word immediate isn't in it! It says, "When you do what is right, God will someday bring good from it." God just holds you responsible for going to make it right. He doesn't hold you responsible for the other person's actions and reactions.

"What if the situation gets worse?" Let me just say, not all situations will work out the way you would like them to work out. Some of the things you go through with the best intentions may result in a worse condition. I can't promise you immediate or even ultimate change. All I can say is that if you go and do what is right, your conscience is clear.

"What if I just take it to God and say, 'God forgive me.'" First of all, it's a contradiction of what Jesus taught in Matthew 5:24. He's not talking about being reconciled to God; He's talking about being reconciled to another person. Why is that important? It's because it's easy to be reconciled to God; it's not as easy to be reconciled to one another. Let me give you an illustration. Let's say that I back out of my driveway and hit my neighbor's car that's parked across the street. And I pray, "Father, forgive me for the way I drive." And then I write a note that says, "Dear neighbor, I hit your car but God has forgiven me," and I leave the note on my neighbor's car. Is that the end of it? Not unless your neighbors are different from mine, because my neighbor is going to contact me to find out what I'm going to do about the damage. Why? It's because I didn't offend God; I offended my neighbor and I've got to go through the hard process of making it right.

All of us have been in situations where we've needed forgiveness and we've experienced the joy that comes with receiving it. We've also been in situations where we were the ones that had to extend forgiveness, and we've all felt the joy that comes with releasing the debt and having a relationship restored. But how do we handle a situation where a person keeps hurting us over and over again?

One day Jesus is talking to a group of people and he's explaining the process that two individuals should go through to restore a relationship that's been broken down. And while Peter is listening, Jesus must have said something that reminded him of something that was going on in his own life. And based on Peter's question for Jesus, I'm assuming that someone had offended Peter, and not just once, but over and over and over again. Peter is listening to what Jesus is teaching, and at the same time, he's thinking about his own personal situation and he's trying to figure out how the two go together. And so when Jesus finishes his lesson, Peter pulls Jesus off to the side and he asks Jesus a question. He asks, "How many times am I required to forgive someone that keeps hurting me over and over again? Where do I get to draw the line?" And to impress Jesus he said, "How about seven times?" And that was a good response because the Torah taught that you were to forgive three times. So, Peter is thinking, "Why don't I go the extra mile? I'll double what the Torah teaches and I'll add one for good measure."

But in asking the question, Peter revealed a common misconception about the nature of forgiveness, and I think that at some point in our lives, most of us have suffered from the same confusion. Peter's assumption is that forgiveness is for the benefit of the offender. In other words, if we want to do something nice and take the high road for the person that hurt us, we will choose to forgive them. So, Peter says, "I'll take the high road; I'll go the extra mile; I'll forgive them seven times. But after the seventh time, do I get to say, 'That's it; I can't do this anymore,'" because Peter was convinced, just as many of us are convinced, that to forgive someone is to do them a favor. Why is that? It's because, when someone wounds us or hurts us, there's always a sense that the person who hurt us is indebted to us. It's as if they've taken something from us, so they've created a debt in the relationship. That's why we say things like, "You owe me an apology." You may feel that your boss owes you recognition and you're going to be mad until you get it. You may feel like your wife owes you respect, so you're angry. You may feel like your husband needs to be more sensitive; he owes it to you, but because he isn't, you're angry. That's the way we think, and as a result, we all develop these debtor relationships. And instead of dealing with the issue and attempting to resolve it, we hold on to it.

And in our minds, we begin to build our case. In fact, we have imaginary conversations with ourselves. Do you ever do that? And those are great conversations to have with ourselves because we always look great and it always ends great. In our mind, we're going to present our case and once the person that offended us sees our side, they'll drop to their knees and beg us for forgiveness. They'll even beg to get back on our good side or in our good graces. I can't tell you how many times I've had those imaginary conversations, but it never actually plays out the way I picture it in my mind. So, until that person comes crawling back to make it right, whenever we're reminded of what happened, we're angry. By the way, the Bible has two words for anger. The first word means, "to grow hot," and the second word means, "pregnant nostrils." Isn't that a great description? When we get angry, our nostrils flare! But in reality, we all have different ways that we display our anger.

Some of us are like a volcano when we get angry. We rumble and rumble and rumble inside. We say things to ourselves like, "I've been taking this from my boss for years; I've had it; today I'm letting him have it." We blast into his or her office and we give our boss a piece of our mind that we can't afford to lose. We spew hot lava and volcanic ash, and when we walk out, all that's left are the charred remains. By the way, one thing I've noticed is that volcanic people never reconcile relationships; they never apologize for being angry.

Others of us take the iceberg approach to dealing with our anger. When someone upsets us, we give them the cold shoulder. And the person that made us angry picks up on it because that's what we want them to do. And they ask us what's wrong and we respond, "Nothing!" And we give them the silent treatment. We ice them out of our lives.

Others of us deal with our anger like a microwave. Maybe you're in a conversation and everything is great, and then someone makes one, little comment. And you push, "Time, Cook, 5 Seconds," and you explode.

My point is that we all struggle with anger. We may express it in different ways, but we all deal with anger. I do. You do. And then one day you're sharing with a close friend how you were hurt and why you have every right to be angry and your friend reminds you that as a Christian, you really shouldn't feel that way and that what you need to do is forgive that person who hurt you. But when someone comes along and says to you, "You need to forgive," it just doesn't make sense, after all you're the victim! And why should you do the offender the favor of forgiving them, when after all, they owe you; you don't owe them. So, you continue to hold onto your anger and your hostility, and you're going to wait it out until they come begging for forgiveness.

The problem is that deep down inside, as a Christian, you

also know you shouldn't feel the way you feel. And so you take all of your emotions and anger and you stuff it down inside, and before you know it, you're depressed and it's because depression is often anger that's been bottled up. And you may think you've dealt with it and it's gone away because you don't talk about it anymore, but it's still there lurking beneath the surface. And maybe that's exactly where Peter was. And Jesus understood his confusion just like He understands our confusion. And so Jesus tells a rather strange story. By the way, if you've read the gospels, you know that Jesus was really good at this. People were always coming up to Jesus to ask simple questions, but instead of just giving simple answers, Jesus would go off on a story. And that's what Jesus does in Matthew; he tells a story.

The story begins in Matthew 18:21-34: "Then Peter came to Jesus and asked, 'Lord, how many times shall I forgive my brother or sister who sins against me? Up to seven times?" Jesus answered, 'I tell you, not seven times, but seventy-seven times. Therefore, the kingdom of heaven is like a king who wanted to settle accounts with his servants. As he began the settlement, a man who owed him ten thousand bags of gold was brought to him. Since he was not able to pay, the master ordered that he and his wife and his children and all that he had be sold to repay the debt. At this the servant fell on his knees before him. 'Be patient with me,' he begged, 'and I will pay back everything.' The servant's master took pity on him, canceled the debt and let him go. But when that servant went out, he found one of his fellow servants who owed him a hundred silver coins. He grabbed him and began to choke him. 'Pay back what you owe me!' he demanded. His fellow servant fell to his knees and begged him, 'Be patient with me, and I will pay it back.' But he refused. Instead, he went off and had the man thrown into prison until he could pay the debt. When the other servants saw what had happened, they were outraged and went and told their master everything that had happened. Then the master called the servant in. 'You wicked servant,' he said, 'I canceled all that debt of yours because you begged me to. Shouldn't you have had mercy on your fellow servant just as I had on you?' In anger his master handed him over to the jailers to be tortured, until he should pay back all he owed."

Now, we don't have any idea what Peter is thinking, but my guess is that halfway into Jesus' story, he realizes, "This isn't going the way I wanted it to go." After all, it's pretty clear to him that God is the king in the story and that means that Peter must be the wicked servant in the story. And he's the one who's been forgiven a lot, but he's also the one who's making a big deal out of not forgiving the guy for what seems, in comparison, a little. And Peter may not have been the brightest bulb in the box, but he got it. He understood that the moral of the story is that he has to forgive every single time he's hurt, and if he doesn't, God is coming after him. And I am confident that his very next thought was the very same thought you're having about now, "That's not fair." And I'm sure that Peter is thinking, "Jesus, you misunderstood; I'm the victim here. And you're telling me that if I don't take the high road and forgive, you're coming after me too? They're after me and you're after me; is that the moral of the story?" But notice how Jesus wraps up the parable in Matthew 18:35: "This is how my Heavenly Father will treat each of you unless you forgive your brother from your heart." Drop the mic. And Peter is thinking, "Next time I'll just keep my questions to myself."

And we smile, but I realize that many who are reading this right now have gone through incredible hurt and pain. And you could tell your story and we'd be so mad and angry at the person that hurt you, and we would also feel that you're justified in being angry and feeling the way you do. But this is what Jesus says, "You've got to forgive or I'm coming after you." And we hear that and think, "How can God say that; I thought He was a good God. Why would He want to add to my misery by being my enemy? I already have an enemy."

Let me give you a couple of reasons why Jesus basically threatens us into forgiving other people: First, God knows that when we refuse to forgive and we choose instead to hold on to anger and hurt and bitterness, it's equivalent to shifting into self-destruct mode; it's just a matter of time. Because when we refuse to cancel the debt and let it go, we chain ourselves to the hurt and we drag it with us everywhere we go. As insensitive as it may seem, God knows that about us and loves us enough to say in no uncertain terms, "Because I love you, you have to forgive or you're going to have to deal with me because I know that if you to refuse to let go of that anger and hurt, it's going to cause you to self-destruct and your life is going to end up a disaster."

Do you know where you see this a lot? You see it with teens. I was recently talking with a high school student and I discovered that she was a good student from a wealthy, and what sounded like, solid family. One day after a few minutes of casual conversation she blurted out, "Sometimes I cut myself." She also shared that she was on medication for anxiety and she had weekly appointments with a therapist. And when she revealed this to me, it broke my heart that this young girl who had her entire life ahead of her was paralyzed by anxiety.

We've all encountered similar individuals. And when you begin to poke around, you discover often that anger is at the root of that person's issues. Maybe they're mad at mom or dad or a friend. In my young friend's case, it was a friend, but she didn't understand how destructive it is to hold on to the anger and so it made her do self-destructive things. And in some twisted way, she cuts herself because she thinks she's getting back at the friend who hurt her. And you hear stories like that and think, "How tragic," but that's what anger looks like when it goes unresolved. Do you know where else you see this? You see it in couples who've been married 20, 25, maybe 30 years, but then their marriage implodes. And when you poke around you discover that there's usually something that happened years ago that's never been forgiven, and that anger that's been repressed for years finally surfaces. And it's not that they didn't have a right to be angry but instead of dealing with it, it's still hanging on and it's destroying the marriage.

Now, as I said earlier, I know that anger is a complex emotion, and Paul helps us learn how to process our anger in Ephesians 4. And we need to be aware of Paul's advice because anger is something that we're going to face every day of our lives. Do you know why? It's because we are going to have to deal with the issue of forgiveness everyday of our lives. And the inability to forgive will always lead to some level of anger.

Pauls begins in Ephesians 4:26: "In your anger, do not sin." As I said earlier, anger is neutral, but when we get angry it can easily lead to sin. This verse reminds us that even when we're angry, we still shouldn't sin. One of the things I've learned about anger is that it's like a trapeze. In other words, anger usually isn't the first emotion that most of us feel; it's usually the second, maybe even third emotion.

As we learned earlier, the story of Joseph is a good example of this. We're told in Genesis that Jacob had twelve sons and he loved his sons, but there was one son who was the apple of his eye and his name was Joseph. In fact, Jacob loved Joseph so much that he made Joseph this designer robe specifically for Joseph. And, as you would expect, Joseph's brothers felt hurt; they were jealous and we can all understand that. But instead of dealing with those feelings of jealousy and hurt, they jumped on the trapeze and swung over those first emotions, and they fell right into the arms of their secondary emotion, anger. And the brothers got so angry, they sold Joseph into slavery. But before we come down too hard on these guys, realize that we do the same thing. We swing over the first emotion because it's often easier to be angry than to deal with the real issues. For example, a husband calls his wife from work and says, "Honey,

I'll be home at 6:00." Then, 6:30 arrives and he's not there; and 7:00 comes and goes and he's still not there. There's no call or text; nothing. And the wife is upset and hurt; she doesn't feel like a priority. But instead of dealing with the real source of hurt because it's too painful, she swings over those feelings and lands right in the arms of anger. Finally, about 7:30, her husband walks through the door, but instead of expressing her real feelings to him, she hits him with a machine gun round of shots. "You're always late; you never think about anyone else, and I cooked a special meal for you." It's like, bam, bam, bam, bam, but it's the second emotion. What is it that you're swinging over in your life? What is it that you are choosing to ignore and not deal with? What's really at the root of your anger? What are you choosing to avoid instead of seeking to resolve?

And then Paul gives us that great insight that helps us make sure that our anger doesn't control us in Ephesians 4:26: "Do not let the sun go down while you are still angry." In other words, we have to learn how to deal with our anger in a timely manner. It's okay to be mad because you've been hurt, but it's not okay to carry your hurt and anger around for so long that it begins to affect your actions and attitude and words. Paul says, "To avoid that, deal with your anger as soon as possible." Why? It's because eventually it's going to cause us to sin. In fact, when we're angry, our sin potential goes through the roof because eventually it will cause us to do and say and decide things that we'll later wish we could undo. But it doesn't stop there because sooner or later, our unresolved anger will begin to spill over into other relationships. Paul says, "You've got to stop that cycle, and the way to do it is to learn to deal with your anger quickly."

But there's another reason this is so crucial, and this explains why hanging onto anger isn't acceptable or tolerable. It's because if we don't deal quickly with our anger in a timely manner, we will eventually forget what made us angry. In other words, if something happens to me and I don't deal with my anger by nightfall, or the next night, or the next month, or the next year, what happens? Eventually my circumstances and environment and scenery changes. Eventually, I'm not around that person or in that relationship anymore. Eventually, I have a different job or a different marriage. But even though my circumstances have changed, if I haven't resolved my anger, I'll carry it with me. And for that very reason, there are a lot of angry people reading this. And if someone were to ask, "What are you so angry about?" you'd probably point to someone in your life right now. Maybe it's a spouse or child or coworker or neighbor. But your real issue lies in a relationship that maybe you've forgotten about or you're now distant from. And because the sun has set so many times, you don't realize, "That's the real source of my anger." And so you're still carrying that anger but you don't know how to resolve it because you're not sure where it came from. And unfortunately, a lot of us operate off the assumption, "All I need is some time and a different environment and I'll be okay. If I can just get out of this marriage or this job or this relationship and change my environment, then I'll be fine." But that's like getting into a car accident and telling the paramedics. "If you'll just get me away from this accident site, I'll be okay." They would never do that, because they know that wherever they take you, you take your injuries and hurt with you.

And in the same way, a lot of you have left some accident scenes in your past. And your thinking is, "Now that I'm away from him and that environment, I'll be okay." But Paul tells us, "That's not the case; you have to deal with it." By the way, you see this often in people who are recently divorced and they're thinking about getting remarried because they've finally met Mr. or Ms. Right. And they're so excited because their ex wasn't a believer, but this new person is a believer and so they assume that everything is going to be great. In fact, they can't wait to start all over again. But let me give you a warning: To move from one hurtful relationship right into another relationship will spell disaster. And it's because if there's unresolved hurt and anger, it will eventually spill over into your new relationship; you can count on it. So, the best thing you can do, as hard as it may be, is to give yourself some time and make sure that God has given you the ability and the grace to forgive that previous spouse who hurt you because the worst thing you can do is carry unresolved anger from one relationship to another. Because even though the scenery has changed, it doesn't mean the hurt has been healed. And only forgiveness and letting go of the anger begins the process.

In fact, Paul tells us why this is so crucial in Ephesians 4:27, "…and do not give the devil a foothold." The word for foothold also means stronghold. In other words, the devil moves into your life in such a way that he has a base of operation. And from that base of operation, he can begin to impact other areas and other relationships in your life. You're giving the devil an opportunity to do that. It's not that he takes it; you give it to him. You're basically saying, "Come on in; happy to have you. Feel free to spread as much chaos as you would like in all of my relationships and life!" So, Paul says, "I know that there are people on your case and bombarding you and attacking you, but you can't allow the sun to set even one time on unresolved anger." That means that we have to forgive and forgive and forgive and forgive some more. And if we have to forgive ten times a day, we forgive ten times a day, but we cannot afford to run the risk of storing up anger because it will give the devil a foothold that will eventually manifest itself in other areas and other relationships in our lives.

So, what do you do about your anger? Paul goes on to say in Ephesians 4:31-32, "Get rid of all bitterness, rage and anger, brawling and slander, along with every form of malice. Be kind and compassionate to one another, forgiving each other just as in Christ God forgave you."

Question! Who in your life do you really have a problem

with? Maybe you have made a habit out of going to bed angry. It's been going on for days, maybe months, maybe years. And as a result, what was a solvable issue at one time has exploded in your life, and it has caused even more issues. And that's why God says to us through this parable in Matthew 18, "I understand your pain and hurt and anger, but you've got to let it go because it's destroying you." Trust me on this, the past will never be the past until you deal with this issue of forgiveness.

But there's a second reason Jesus had the guts to say what he said on that day. Jesus knew that in a few days he was going to die on the cross and it was going to change the course of history. This is what Paul wrote in 2 Corinthians 5:21: "God made him who had no sin to be sin for us, so that in him we might become the righteousness of God." By the way, did you know that when Jesus decided to go to the cross for us that he was already aware of all the sins that we would commit in our lives? He already knew about all the promises we would make that we wouldn't follow through on. He already knew about all the times we would fall asleep while praying. He already knew about all the times that we would intentionally disobey. He already knew about the times we would get into trouble and beg Him to bail us out, and then we'd go on our merry little way and forget about His grace and mercy. But do you know what He decided? He decided to forgive us anyway. In other words, He went to the cross knowing exactly what we'd be like, but He did it anyway. And it's in the shadow of the cross that we're commanded to forgive one another. And when you understand this truth, all of the, "but you don't know what they did," becomes insignificant because God hasn't asked us to die for anybody; He just asked us to cancel their debt. And no matter how deep the pain and hurt, we have all lost our right to refuse to forgive because of what Jesus did on the cross to forgive us.

Jesus said to this group and to us, "If you refuse to forgive regardless of how deep the hurt, you're like the wicked servant."

He says, "Think about the mercy you've been shown, and then take that same mercy that you've been shown and show it to the people in your life; cancel their debt. And I know what some of you are thinking: "But you don't know what they've done!" Jesus says, "Yes I do; and I also know what you've done, but I still forgave you."

By the way, this is where we get it all messed up; we want it both ways. We want God to show us mercy, but we want Him to show everyone who has hurt us, justice. In other words, we want them to get what they deserve, but we don't want to get what we deserve. But God says, "You can't have it both ways." Jesus said in Matthew 18:33: "Shouldn't you have had mercy on your fellow servant just as I had on you; not for their sake, but for your sake?"

Sometime back I was incredibly hurt by something that happened in my personal life. But I wasn't just hurt; I was angry and it was affecting my life in a negative way. But then one day I realized that there's really nothing the person who hurt me could ever do to repay the debt. There was nothing they could ever do or say that would undo the hurt, so why hold on to it? So, I canceled the debt and I write this a free man.

You see, forgiveness isn't for the person that hurt you, although it may do some good relationally. Forgiveness is for you. Forgiveness allows you to cut the chain with the past. Forgiveness allows us to move past the anger that eventually impacts all of our relationships. And God knows this so well, He says to us, "You must forgive for your own good, and you must forgive because I forgave you, and when you forgive, you'll be free.'

Now, we've all heard people say, "I'll forgive, but I'll never forget," which makes me question, "Did you really forgive." But that brings up an even better question, "Is it possible to really forgive and forget?" After all, one of the greatest of God's creations is the human mind, especially as you think about the memory aspect. It's more powerful than any computer that will ever be created. In fact, some scientists would argue that we never really forget anything. If that is true, how can anyone forget an offense? To answer that question, we need to look at four passages of Scripture. I'll spend very little time on the first three, but I'll spend significant time on the fourth.

The first one is Psalm 119:165: "Great peace have those who love your law, and nothing can make them stumble." In other words, those who love God's Word as they should, won't even remember an offense long enough to lose their peace. But that verse sounds like a contradiction to the idea that we never really forget anything, but maybe it's not a contradiction at all.

Jesus said in Matthew 7:1-5: "Do not judge, or you too will be judged. For in the same way you judge others, you will be judged, and with the measure you use, it will be measured to you. Why do you look at the speck of sawdust in your brother's eye and pay no attention to the plank in your own eye? How can you say to your brother, 'Let me take the speck out of your eye,' when all the time there is a plank in your own eye? You hypocrite, first take the plank out of your own eye, and then you will see clearly to remove the speck from your brother's eye."

And some of you are thinking, "What does that have to do with memory?" Actually, it has a lot to do with memory. Jesus is saying, "Guard against being negative and small and nitpicking with others." In other words, "Set those things aside; put them out of your mind because, if you don't, you will never be able to get close to anyone. You will write everyone off as not being worthy of a relationship."

The third passage is in I Corinthians 13:4-5: "Love is patient, love is kind. It does not envy, it does not boast, it is not proud. It does not dishonor others, it is not self-seeking, it is not easily angered, it keeps no record of wrongs." Forgetting breaks the lead pencil in your bookkeeping mind. Love comes along and snaps the pencil in two and tosses it aside. It refuses to keep a ledger on someone else. Amy Carmichael wrote: "If I say, 'Yes I forgive but I cannot forget,' as though the God who twice a day washes all the sands of all the shores of all the world could not wash such memories from my mind, then I know nothing of Calvary love. If the One who made the tide that washes the shore cannot wash away from my mind, the caustic remarks and the wrongs of someone else, then I haven't even entered into Calvary love."

I've always thought that we remember the wrong things. The very things we should forget, we remember. The very things we should remember, we continually forget.

If I could wrap all this together and give you a general statement about forgetting, I believe God is saying this: "Forgetting means I disregard an offense again and again and I keep no score of wrong." I don't recall it; I don't repeat it. Webster defines forgetting as, "to treat with inattention or disregard; to put something out of one's mind, to ignore." All of those things are part of the spiritual discipline of forgetting. It requires that we continually disregard and push aside the wrong done against us. It's getting the snags out of our minds so that the truth of God can run freely and have free course. In other words, it's a decision of the will.

We've already recognized in this book that the Apostle Paul was a phenomenal man. He was a superstar as a rabbi. He had a brilliant mind. He had amazing zeal and passion. He was the epitome of what Judaism stood for. But then he met Jesus and suddenly those things dissolved into insignificance. In fact, this is what Paul wrote in Philippians 3:4-7: "If someone else thinks they have reasons to put confidence in the flesh, I have more: circumcised on the eighth day, of the people of Israel, of the tribe of Benjamin, a Hebrew of Hebrews; in regard to the law, a Pharisee; as for zeal, persecuting the church; as for righteousness based on the law, faultless. But whatever were gains to me I now consider loss for the sake of Christ." Now, does that mean that Paul erased all of those things from his mind? Obviously it doesn't because he just listed them for us. It means that he disregarded them; he set them aside; he didn't count them as valuable. Some of us need to do that with education. Some of us need to do that with our achievements. We continually want to put the spotlight on those things and either directly or indirectly refer to how successful we are. But Paul says, "I don't want to do that anymore."

And if you keep reading you'll discover some things that helped Paul pull it off in Philippians 3:7-11: "But whatever were gains to me I now consider loss for the sake of Christ. What is more, I consider everything a loss because of the surpassing worth of knowing Christ Jesus my Lord, for whose sake I have lost all things. I consider them garbage, that I may gain Christ and be found in him, not having a righteousness of my own that comes from the law, but that which is through faith in Christ—the righteousness that comes from God on the basis of faith. I want to know Christ—yes, to know the power of his resurrection and participation in his sufferings, becoming like him in his death, and so, somehow, attaining to the resurrection from the dead."

For many of us, it blows our minds to think that there will be a day when there will be a literal resurrection. Our bodies will be changed; we will no longer have an old sin nature and we will consciously be taken to be with Jesus. For the first time, we will be without the old anchors that hold us down in this life. We will be without remorse and guilt and sorrow and sin and shame and disgrace. We will be rid of all of those things and we will be with Jesus face to face. Paul says, "But I'm not there yet." In fact, Paul says in Philippians 3:12-13: "Not that I have already obtained all this, or have already arrived at my goal, but I press on to take hold of that for which Christ Jesus took hold of me. Brothers and sisters, I do not consider myself yet to have taken hold of it." Paul makes a very vulnerable statement three times. He basically says, "I'm not a model of all of these things," and he implies, "I never will be as long as I'm on this earth."

And now God begins to show us the path to forgetfulness. It begins by being vulnerable, and this is going to be a very hard pill for some to swallow. It's very difficult for many people to say, "I have not obtained; I'm not perfect; I don't regard myself as having laid hold of this standard." To make statements like that takes great vulnerability. What do I mean by vulnerability? Well, several things come to mind.

1st: A quick willingness to declare need.

2nd: An open admonition of wrong and limitations.

3rd: A teachable spirit to learn from anyone, anytime.

4th: A reluctance to appear as the expert.

I've observed over the years that those who lack vulnerability are able to forget their own wrongs, but they have a tough time forgetting the wrongs of others. Are you vulnerable? Would those closest to you use that word to describe you? Vulnerability opens the door for forgetting because it means that I have things that need to be forgotten as well.

Paul continues in Philippians 3:13: "Brothers and sisters, I do not consider myself yet to have taken hold of it. But one thing I do: Forgetting what is behind…" By the way, Paul isn't saying that he erased his past because, as I said, he lists all of his accomplishments just a few verses earlier. Paul is saying that he discarded the significance of it; he consciously set it aside.

Some of you have been deeply hurt and perhaps the hurt has been related to your family. Maybe it's related to a close personal relationship that you haven't been able to patch up or bridge back together. Earlier we looked into the life of Joseph, but allow me to unpack his story a little more. When he was seventeen, he was sold into slavery, forgotten by his family, and hated by his brothers. He had to adjust to a foreign culture. He was later tossed into prison and mistreated. He finally got a job as a servant in the home of Potiphar, and Potiphar's wife busted a move on Joseph but Joseph refused her. She, in turn, accused Joseph of hitting on her and her husband believed her and Joseph ended up back in prison where he stayed until he was thirty. One day God gave Joseph great wisdom and he interpreted Pharaoh's dreams and suddenly Joseph was catapulted into prominence; he became the Prime Minister of Egypt. All of that happened before he was thirty. I think it's safe to say that Joseph had a lot to forget. But I want you to see something in Genesis 41:46-51: "Joseph was thirty years old when he entered the service of Pharaoh king of Egypt. And Joseph went out from Pharaoh's presence and traveled throughout Egypt. During the seven years of abundance the land produced plentifully. Joseph collected all the food produced in those seven years of abundance in Egypt and stored it in the cities. In each city he put the food grown in the fields surrounding it. Joseph stored up huge quantities of grain, like the sand of the sea; it was so much that he stopped keeping records because it was beyond measure. Before the years of famine came, two sons were born to Joseph by Asenath daughter of Potiphera, priest of On. Joseph named his firstborn Manasseh and said, 'It is because God has made me forget all my trouble and all my father's household.'"

And some of you are thinking, "If Joseph would have been hurt the way I've been hurt, he wouldn't be able to forget!" Well, let me correct your thinking. Joseph didn't forget based on his own efforts; God made him forget. In fact, it goes on to say in Genesis 41:52: "The second son he named Ephraim and said, "It is because God has made me fruitful in the land of my suffering." In other words, "Not only have I been able to forget all of the bad stuff that's happened in my life, I've also been productive in the very land where I was afflicted." What a different perspective! Compare that to when you share your hurt with others. Often you will hear the response, "You'll never fully get over that; you're a victim." You're not a victim! In fact, Joseph names his children to remind him of the grace of God in his life.

Let's be honest, some of the deepest wounds we experience

are wounds related to the broken marriages of our past, or the loss of a mate, or the shame of a childhood. God says in Isaiah 54:4-5 says: "Do not be afraid; you will not be put to shame. Do not fear disgrace; you will not be humiliated. You will forget the shame of your youth and remember no more the reproach of your widowhood. For your Maker is your husband — the Lord Almighty is his name—the Holy One of Israel is your Redeemer; he is called the God of all the earth." Wow! What is the mercy and grace of God if it's not that? Why do we spend our time focusing on the very things that God is working so hard to erase? Why do we remind others about the very things that they are trying to forget having been forgiven by God? My heart breaks to see so many in the family of God remembering the things that God says are cast aside.

And so from Paul, we see a statement of vulnerability, "I haven't obtained or arrived." We also see a statement of determination, "I press on." You see it in Philippians 3:14: "I press on toward the goal to win the prize for which God has called me heavenward in Christ Jesus." By the way, that's the same guy who wrote this from a dungeon just before he was beheaded in 2 Timothy 4:7-8: "I have fought the good fight, I have finished the race, I have kept the faith. Now there is in store for me the crown of righteousness, which the Lord, the righteous Judge, will award to me on that day—and not only to me, but also to all who have longed for his appearing." Paul's focus was always on the future. When you get hung up with things that need to be forgiven and forgotten, you will never be productive as it relates to the future; you will be chained to your past. You must go on; you must press on. It's the principle of determination.

Let me wrap up this chapter with three practical responses to this idea of forgiving and forgetting.

1st: Forgetting reminds me that I too have flaws that if others remembered, I would never make it. I wonder how many of us would speak to one another if we knew all there is to know about each other? Do you know what would be incredible? Us knowing everything there is to know about each other and then choosing to forget it. That's really where the rubber meets the road. Not, "not knowing" and accepting, but "knowing" and accepting.

2nd: Forgiving enables me to be big and encouraging, not petty and negative. Some time ago I was approached by an individual who had heard a negative rumor about a person in the church where I was serving. They asked me if I was aware of the situation. My response was, "I know something bad about everybody I know," and so do you, but do we really want to focus on that? Is that how we want to live our lives? I don't think so. What if we all decided that we were never going to write people off? Would our relationships change? Would our churches change? Yes and yes! Our churches would immediately become hospitals for hurting, broken people.

3rd: Forgetting frees me to live for tomorrow instead of being hung up on yesterday. Some of you are reading this and thinking right now, "Where were you when I needed this." Well, it's never too late to start moving in the right direction. When God asks us to forgive and forget, God asks a big thing from us. While God expects a big thing from us, so do all the people we rub shoulders with everyday who are scared to death to admit how much they're hurting. May the Spirit of God, in some beautiful, permanent and personal manner, open a new door in each of our lives as we choose, not only to forgive, but to also forget.

I know that this is a tough topic to grasp and to wrap our heads around. On my journey, I know that many have struggled with forgiving me because of what I did. I know that I have struggled with forgiving many because of the way the situation was handled. I also know that the toughest part of this has been forgiving myself. I have heard it said that often the last person we can forgive is ourselves. I have found that to be true. It's tough, difficult, painful work. But, now we discover that forgiving isn't enough; we also are expected to forget. That's how we find and experience true freedom "from" our pasts. That's how we move forward.

Now, there's nowhere in this chapter where I said that this was an easy thing to do. I actually think that forgiving and forgetting is one of the most difficult challenges we have to deal with in this life, but this is what is helping me (and I say "helping" because it's not the entire solution). When the Great Accuser, Satan brings people to my mind that I have already gone through the process of forgiving, myself included, and that resentment and anger begins to creep in again, I respond to Satan by saying out loud, "I distinctly remember forgiving that person...I distinctly remember forgiving that person...I distinctly remember forgiving that person..." or, "I distinctly remember forgiving those guys.." or, "I distinctly remember forgiving myself..." I think that's what Paul had in mind in 2 Corinthians 10:5, "We demolish arguments and every pretension that sets itself up against the knowledge of God, and we take captive every thought to make it obedient to Christ." That's my goal; that's where I want to be, but I haven't arrived at my destination yet. I'm learning that it's a journey. I still battle resentment, even anger on a regular basis, both with others and with myself, but it is lessening everyday. And I'm praying that by practicing the truth of 2 Corinthians 10:5 and taking every thought captive, one day I will be able to say like Joseph in Genesis 41:51: "It is because God has made me forget all my trouble..." And as a result, I will be able to unchain myself from the past and move forward...free. I hope you can find and experience that freedom too.

Chapter 8

"I Get By With a Little Help From My Friends!"

I want to begin this chapter by addressing the question, "What does biblical restoration really look like?" and, to do that I want us to once again visit the familiar story of the prodigal Son that Jesus told in Luke 15. Earlier in the book we looked at this story from the perspective of the older brother and we talked about what legalism looks like and how destructive it can be when it comes to restoring individuals. Oddly enough, we can also learn what biblical restoration looks like from the same story.

As I said earlier, the story of the prodigal is the most familiar parable Jesus ever told. It's about a young man who received his inheritance from his father, but he squandered it all away. And when he finally hit rock bottom, we read in Luke 15:16: He longed to fill his stomach with the pods that the pigs were eating, but no one gave him anything. And when I read the end of that verse, I always think of the father, because you know that there hasn't been one sunset since that boy left home that this dad hasn't looked on the horizon for his son's silhouette. You know that not one sunset has come and gone without that father praying for his son's safe return. If you are the parent of a wayward child, you understand.

But thankfully we read in Luke 15:17-18: "When he came to his senses he said, 'How many of my father's hired servants have food to spare, and here I am starving to death. I will set out and go back to my father and say to him...,'" And he starts thinking through how he's going to explain how he ended up in this mess. By the way, some lessons are never learned without a hungry stomach. Some things are never learned without the news of a disease. Some things about life, respect and godliness are never learned without experiencing the pigpen. I'm speaking from experience; I've been there; I know what I'm talking about. And that's where this boy finds himself. He's learned his lesson, but he's had to learn it the hard way.

And the story continues in Luke 15:20: "So, he got up and went to the Father." And I don't think that the thought ever crossed his mind that the father wouldn't welcome him back. I came across this quote: "When sheep are lost, you go hunt for them. When coins are lost, you sweep until you find them. But when a son is lost, you wait until he comes home." And that's exactly what this father has done; he's patiently waited. And finally, one day he sees that gaunt silhouette against the evening sun, and he realizes, "He's home."

Now remember, this father doesn't know what his son has been up to. He's not aware of his lifestyle. He doesn't know that his son has squandered all of his money. He doesn't know that the boy has prepared a speech. He doesn't know that the boy has come to his senses. He's never read Luke 15. He doesn't know how the story's going to end. But it says in Luke 15:20: "But while he was still a long way off, his father saw him and was filled with compassion for him; he ran to his son, threw his arms around him and kissed him."

Now, let's be honest, that's not how most Christians would have responded. Instead we set up systems of probation. We say things like, "Let's keep an eye on him for a while and if he doesn't screw up, again, maybe we'll welcome him back!" That's not God's style when it comes to restoration. All it takes is for the son to say, "Father, forgive me," and our Father is all over us. He takes us back instantly. So, while this father is all over the son, it says in Luke 15:21: "The Son said to him, 'Father I have sinned against heaven and against you. I am no longer worthy to be called your son.'" And he couldn't even finish the speech he'd prepared. Luke 15:21 says, "But the Father said to the servants, 'Quick! Bring the best robe and put it on him. Put a ring on his finger and sandals on his feet.'" And these gifts are significant because these are also three gifts that the Father gives each one of us as his children, and so I want to talk about what these gifts represent. But to do that, we need to look at a lot of Old Testament scriptures to give us some history and perspective.

First, the father gave the son a robe, but what does that mean to us today as Christians? Well, my guess is that we all get dressed physically every morning before we leave the house, but do you also get dressed spiritually? Have you ever left the house spiritually naked because you chose not to put your robe on? In this story of the prodigal, the father gave the son a robe, but it was up to the son to put it on. In the same way, God has given us a robe to put on every day. What kind of robe has He given us to put on? Isaiah 61:10: "I delight greatly in the Lord; for my soul rejoices in my God. For he has clothed me with garments of salvation and arrayed me in a robe of righteousness." So, this verse tells us that the robe our Father has given us is a robe of righteousness. Zechariah 3:3 is another example: "Now Joshua was clothed with filthy clothes..." By the way, this is the same word used in Isaiah 64:6: "...all of our righteous acts are like filthy rags." And the term "filthy rags" is a reference to our attempt to be righteous. Righteous simply means, "right standing with God." Think about the best day you've ever had spiritually. Maybe you went to church and while you were there you worshiped passionately, you gave generously and you served selflessly. On top of that you fasted and you prayed for three hours and you read through the entire Book of Leviticus, plus you helped a little old lady cross the street. That's a good day! But the best we can do on our best day will never put us in a right standing with God. Only accepting what Jesus did for us on the cross can put us in a right standing with God.

Back to Zechariah 3:3-4: "Now Joshua was dressed in filthy clothes as he stood before the angel. The angel said to those who were standing before him, 'Take off his filthy clothes.' Then he said to Joshua, 'See I have taken away your sin, and I will put fine garments (also translated "robes") on you.'" And this is again a reference to the fact that God removes our sin and covers us with a robe of righteousness. He takes away our attempt at righteousness and He gives us his righteousness. But let me add, as a Christian, I can choose to live a righteous life led by the Spirit, or I can choose to live an unrighteous life. And if I chose to live an unrighteous life, it's like running around spiritually naked; it brings shame to God, to me, and to the Body of Christ. So, let me ask you, are you wearing your robe the Father gave you; are you putting it on everyday? What would that look like? Colossians 3:12-14 says: "Therefore, as God's chosen people, holy and dearly loved, clothe yourselves with compassion, kindness, humility, gentleness and patience. Bear with each other and forgive one another if any of you has a grievance against someone. Forgive as the Lord forgave you. And over all these virtues put on love, which binds them all together in perfect unity." So, you have a robe; are you wearing it? That's the first gift that God gives us when He restores us.

Second, the Father gave the son a ring. I want to show a verse to help you understand what the ring represents. Genesis 41:42-43 says: "Then Pharaoh took his signet ring from his finger and put it on Joseph's finger. He dressed him in robes of fine linen and put a gold chain around his neck. He had him ride in a chariot as his second-in-command, and men shouted before him, 'Make way!' Thus he put him in charge of the whole land of Egypt." So, what does the ring represent in the Bible? The ring represents authority. When Pharaoh gave Joseph his ring, it meant that Pharaoh had given Joseph his authority. But let me explain something about authority; it's also assigned; it's given.

In other words, the only reason that Joseph had authority was because Pharaoh gave or assigned it to him. In the same way, we don't have authority on our own; we have authority because God gave us his authority.

In Matthew 21, we learn something about this authority that's very important. Matthew 21:23-31 says: "Jesus entered the temple courts, and, while he was teaching, the chief priests and the elders of the people came to him. 'By what authority are you doing these things?' they asked. 'And who gave you this authority?' Jesus replied, 'I will also ask you one question. If you answer me, I will tell you by what authority I am doing these things. John's baptism—where did it come from? Was it from heaven, or of human origin?' They discussed it among themselves and said, 'If we say, "From heaven," he will ask, "Then why didn't you believe him?" But if we say, "Of human origin"—we are afraid of the people, for they all hold that John was a prophet.' So, they answered Jesus, 'We don't know.' Then He said, 'Neither will I tell you by what authority I am doing these things.' What do you think? There was a man who had two sons. He went to the first and said, "Son, go and work today in the vineyard." "I will not," he answered, but later he changed his mind and went. Then the father went to the other son and said the same thing. He answered, "I will, sir," but he did not go. 'Which of the two did what his father wanted?' 'The first,' they answered. Jesus said to them, 'Truly I tell you, the tax collectors and the prostitutes are entering the kingdom of God ahead of you.'"

Now, the original question was, "Where does your authority come from?" and then Jesus tells them this parable, so what was He saying? He was saying that the authority comes by obeying the Father. So, when I ask, "Are you wearing your ring?" I'm really asking, "Are you living under God's authority?" Because if you're not, your authority is in jeopardy.

Here's the $64,000 question: Why do we need authority; why

is it so important? Jesus said in Matthew 28:18-19, "'All authority in heaven and earth has been given to me. Therefore, go and make disciples.'" So, in Matthew 28, Jesus gave His followers the authority, but they didn't have the power. A few weeks later in Acts 1:8, Jesus said, "You shall receive power." Jesus was saying to his disciples, "I am going to send the Holy Spirit to you, and when the Holy Spirit arrives on the scene, not only will you have the authority, you will also have the power." And Acts 2 tells us that on the day of Pentecost, sure enough, the power fell on those 120 people gathered in that upper room, and then Peter went out into the streets of Jerusalem and preached that great message. And 3,000 were added to that first church that day and the gospel began to ripple throughout the world until the church has become what it is today. How could that possibly happen? It happened because they were operating under the authority and power of Jesus Christ.

If the church of Jesus Christ is going to change the world, it will require us to live and operate under the same authority. And why is this so important? It's because it's foolish to think that Satan is just going to sit back and allow us to reach the world for Jesus Christ. So, we also need authority because there's a spiritual battle going on. Satan and his demons are real and we are involved in a spiritual battle that's real. Despite what you've been told, or read, or think, they're real; they exist, and they want to destroy your marriage and your family. They want to destroy you. Their goal is to short-circuit everything we desire to do for the Kingdom of God. But we don't need to be afraid because God has given us the authority over Satan and his demons. He's given us His authority. He's given us the ring. James 4:7 says, "Submit yourselves, then, therefore to God. Resist the devil, and he will flee from you." 1 John 4:4 says, "You, dear children, are from God and have overcome them (Satan and his demons), because the one who is in you is greater than the one who is in the world." 1 Peter 5:9 says, "Resist him, standing firm in the faith…" How do you stand firm in the faith? You learn and apply the Word of God in your life; you hide it in your heart. You spend that crucial time in prayer. 1 Peter 5:9 continues, "Resist him, standing firm in the faith, because you know that your brothers throughout the world are undergoing the same kind of sufferings." You've been given the authority to resist Satan's power, but you have to wear the ring of authority that the Father gave you; you have to live in obedience. But if you choose not to live in obedience, you're vulnerable. And that may explain why you are having problems in certain areas of your life.

Third, the Father gave the son shoes. What do the shoes represent? Do you remember the story of Boaz and Ruth? In the story, Ruth's husband died and she became a widow, but in Ruth's day, God established a law to help Jewish widows who were left without an heir. God established this idea of the family redeemer. The family redeemer was a close living relative and he had a couple of responsibilities. First, he was to manage the estate that was left. Second, if it was appropriate, he could marry the widow. That's the law of the family redeemer, sometimes referred to as the kinsman redeemer. Well, through a series of circumstances, Boaz meets Ruth and falls in love with her, but Boaz discovers that he's second in line as the kinsman redeemer. So, he goes to the first guy in line and asks, "Are you going to marry Ruth?" And the relative says, "No." And so Boaz responds, "Then I'll marry her because I'm next in line." And the first guy in line said, "Go for it." We pick up the story on Ruth 4:7: "(Now in earlier times in Israel, for the redemption and transfer of property to become final, one party took off his sandal and gave it to the other. This was the method of legalizing transactions in Israel)." And so the first guy gives his sandal to Boaz; it was a legal transaction. It was this guy's way of saying that he was giving up his right to marry Ruth; he gave up his shoe. Think about it: what did God tell Moses to do at the burning bush? He told him

to take his shoes off. What was he saying to Moses? He was saying, "Give up your rights." What did the angel tell Joshua before
the battle of Jericho? He told him to take off his shoes. Why? He
was saying, "Give up your rights; you're not the commander. If
you want to win this battle, I'm in charge." So, taking off your
shoes means that you are giving up your rights.

But what are the benefits of putting on shoes? First, shoes
protect us. Now, if you're reading this and you're a female, your
response may be different. Your response is probably, "Shoes
complete the outfit," and you would be right also. Shoes do complete the outfit. This is what Paul said when he was describing
the armor of God in Ephesians 6:13-15: "Therefore put on the
full armor of God, so that when the day of evil comes, you may
be able to stand your ground, and after you have done everything, to stand. Stand firm then, with the belt of truth buckled
around your waste, with the breastplate of righteousness in
place, and with your feet fitted with the readiness that comes
from the gospel of peace."

Second, shoes give us confidence. What happens when you
give a kid a new pair of Nikes? They try to show you how fast
they can run and how high they can jump! Why? It's because
their new shoes give them new confidence. In the same way, our
spiritual shoes give us confidence. They remind me that I'm a
child of the Father.

Third, shoes give us freedom. For example, in the Old Testament, the first thing they did when they captured slaves was to
remove their shoes. It was a sign; slaves didn't have shoes. That's
why when the prodigal came home and he said, "Make me a
servant," the Father responded, "No way; give that boy some
shoes; he's my son!" So, shoes give us freedom.

As children of God, when we come home from the pigpen,
our Heavenly Father gives us a robe and a ring and a pair of new
shoes. That's what biblical restoration looks like. That's the attitude with which God restores us. He restores our position, our

authority, our protection, our confidence, and our freedom to be the person he created us to be. It's called redemption, and that is also the attitude that he expects us to have when it comes to restoring one another. Does that resemble how most of the Christians you know respond when a prodigal returns home? Does that sound like your Christian friends? Does that reflect the attitude of the church you attend? If it does, then you are in a church that's positioned to impact its community and the world, but you're also in a very special church because it will attract broken and hurting people. It will be a magnet for the downcast and dejected.

Now, I'll let you in on a secret that's kind of an unspoken understanding among Christians. Ready? It's okay to raise hell and be a real extravagant sinner as long as you're an outsider who's never been an insider. In fact, the more extravagant the sin, the better! And the reason that it's okay is because if you ever decide to follow Jesus, you'll make a great story. Churches will interview you and video your story. If the sin is extravagant enough, you may even get a book or movie deal offered to you. But once you've been on the inside and you screw-up, you can kiss that kind of forgiveness and acceptance good-bye, because now when you sin, you're making us all look bad. And no matter how much you repent and no matter how sorry you are, it's going to be on your permanent record. Trust me, that would be the typical church position. The problem is, I don't think that Jesus held the same position on this issue of restoration. After all, He's the one who said that it's not the healthy that need a doctor or a hospital, it's the sick. One of my big frustrations with Christians is that when a fellow Christian stumbles, how we typically respond looks nothing like how the father responded in the story of the prodigal. And I think it's because most Christians feel that when someone screws up big time, there has to be justice. And justice means that the individual has to get what he or she deserves; and that may be your attitude.

When we live like that, we need to understand that it doesn't reflect the heart of God. I mean, we've all heard it said that as Christians, we're supposed to love the sinner and hate the sin. And I don't know about you, but I've found that to be easy to do as long as I'm not relationally connected to the one doing the sinning, and as long as the sin that the person is involved with hasn't touched my life. But how do you handle it when the sinner is someone that you're in a relationship with? How do you handle it when it's someone you had high expectations for? How do you handle it when they do something that costs you your time and money? My guess is that you handle it the same way I do. We suddenly feel like we have to take some kind of action. Maybe we need to convict, or point something out, or somehow punish them. After all, if we don't do something, the person will just think that everything is okay, or maybe they'll think they got away with their bad behavior and so it's our job to make sure that they suffer some. Plus, if we just love and accept them where they are, they'll think that we approve and accept their actions.

My point is, it's easy to love the sinner and hate the sin when the sin doesn't touch us directly, but when it does, our lives are flooded with all kinds of emotions. Sometimes we feel anger. Sometimes we feel disappointment or frustration. Sometimes we feel grief or sorrow. Sometimes we feel all sorts of things that we didn't even know we could feel. And the tendency for those of us who've been Christians for a while is to grab some verse and somehow work it into the conversation. If you're a parent you say to your child, "Don't you remember…?" If you're a child and it's your parent that's screwed up, you remind them of something they taught you as a child. And you throw it up at them and say, "Don't you remember…?" But when someone we're in a relationship with goes prodigal and makes a bad decision, it's never an emotionally neutral environment; with all of the emotions, it's really hard to love the sinner and hate the sin. The great news is that God's Word addresses this very tension. And so I want us to look at a section of the Bible that maybe you've read before or maybe you haven't. In this passage, the Apostle Paul answers this question, "What do you do when someone you love goes prodigal and chooses behavior that you consider to be wrong?" Or maybe they make a bad decision that hurts you financially or relationally. Maybe it hurts your reputation. How do you do the right thing without making the situation worse? How do you make sure that not only the prodigal returns home, but he or she stays home? How do you make sure that, like in the story, full restoration takes place?

In Paul's letter to the Galatians, he addresses this topic of restoration by saying in Galatians 6:1, "Brothers and sisters, if someone is caught in a sin…" And when Paul uses that phrase, "caught in a sin," he doesn't mean that you walked into the bedroom and caught them in the act. The word caught refers to someone who's entangled or ensnared. In other words, they are caught up in a sin. And so Paul spells out in Galatians 6:1: "Brothers and sisters, if someone is caught in a sin, you who live by the Spirit…" And that's not a sappy term that Paul uses for the spiritual elite. He's talking about any believer who's committed to living the Christian life. He's talking about the average Christian who's just trying to get it right, and we know that's what he means because Paul uses this term in other places throughout the New Testament. So, Paul continues in Galatians 6:1 to say, "When someone you know is caught up in a sin, those of you who aren't caught up in that sin…should restore him." He doesn't say, "Ignore them," or "Judge them," or "Punish them." But I can promise you this, if you're in a relationship with someone and they've chosen a lifestyle that's hurt you, you had an emotion that made you either want to stand back and judge them, or walk away and ignore them, or get involved and punish them. Do you know why? It's because it brings stuff to the surface that we don't even like to admit is inside of us. Paul adds a little word at the end of Galatians 6:1: "Brothers and sisters, if someone is caught in a sin, you who live by the Spirit should restore that person gently." Why does Paul add the word, gently? It's because he knows that it's our nature to say, "I'm right; you're wrong, and you're at my mercy because it's me and God against you." And we've all had those conversations, especially if you're a parent. Paul reminds us that the agenda isn't to punish, ignore, or judge. The agenda is to restore, and to do that, we have to put on the emotional breaks and do it gently.

Do you know why? It's because one of the emotions you experience when someone close to you does something wrong is anger. And do you know why you're angry? You're angry because they're not doing what you think they ought to do, or they're not doing what you raised them to do. They're not doing what you thought they would do in that situation. They're not acting right and it ticks you off. And if you've been a Christian a long time and you've learned the system, you'll say, "I'm not angry because they're not doing what I want them to do; I'm angry because they're not doing what God wants them to do." Liar! And do you know how I know you're lying? Think about the anger that surfaces in you when someone else sins and compare that to the anger that surfaces in you when you sin. Let's be honest, isn't it much easier to get the whole self-righteous thing going when it's somebody else that screwed up? That's why Paul says, "When someone that you're in a relationship with hurts you, regardless of who it is or what that person has done, the goal is restoration. That's the target. That's the destination...and you've got to go there gently."

Then he goes on to say in Galatians 6:1: "...if someone is caught in a sin, you who live by the Spirit should restore that person gently. But watch yourselves..." And we read that and think, "Why do I need to watch myself? It's me and God and the Holy Spirit. It's the other person who needs to be watching out!" But Paul tells us why he says, "but watch yourselves," in the last part of Galatians 6:1: "But watch yourselves, or you also may be tempted." The word watch means to examine. And once again Paul turns the focus on us and it bothers us because we're thinking, "It's not me that's wrong, he's the one that's wrong; she's the one that's wrong!" Paul says, "Be careful; remember that the goal is restoration. And if you don't go in gently and if you don't go in examining yourself, you won't restore. Instead, you'll judge or ignore or punish. You'll quote the Bible and you'll be right, but you won't restore, and if you don't restore, you've failed."

By the way, what does Paul mean when he says, "Examine yourself so you won't be tempted?" I used to think that it meant that I needed to be careful so I didn't fall into the same temptation. For example, if my friend is in a bar, drunk as a fish, I need to be careful when I go into the bar to rescue him or I may be tempted and start drinking and end up drunk as a fish too! That's not what Paul is talking about. He's saying that when someone close to us hurts us, it brings all kinds of crud to the surface of our lives. For example, do you know what always surfaces? Pride. And pride sounds like this: "I can't believe you would treat your own dad that way." Or, "I can't believe that you would put me at risk that way." Or, "I can't believe that you would be so insensitive to me." Or, "I can't believe how you're treating me." So, Paul says, "You've got to watch yourself, because when you're hurt, even when the other person is wrong, something ugly in you is going to surface. And if you act on the pride, you'll fall into temptation."

Do you know what else surfaces? Insecurity. And we ask questions like, "What are people going to say when they find out that my daughter is pregnant?" Or, "What are people going to say when they find out that my son has a drug problem?" Or, "What are people going to say when they find out that my spouse cheated?" Insecurities surface in us that we didn't even know we had. So, Paul says, "You've got to step back and cool down. You may clearly be right and the other person may clearly be wrong; you may have every reason to be hurt. But before you go charging in, remember that the goal is restoring the person with their Heavenly Father. And if you don't deal with what surfaces in you, you may ignore and judge and punish, but you won't make any progress toward restoration." In fact, when you respond out of anger, or pride, or insecurity, you'll do more damage than good. You'll actually drive the person further away.

Paul continues by giving us the "how to" of restoration in Galatians 6:2: "Carry each other's burdens..." Let me tell you what that means, and I'll warn you ahead of time, this is extremely convicting. Paul says that you restore by your own action of taking on the complications and the consequences caused by the person's sin. To which we respond, "I don't think so! I've got my own life and my own family and my own financial problems. You're telling me that this bozo messes up and complicates my life and I'm supposed to waltz into their situation and say, 'Let me help you?'" But notice the rest of Galatians 6:2: "...and in this way you will fulfill the law of Christ." Do you know what Paul is saying? He's saying, "Remember that while you were still a sinner, Christ didn't punish you or judge you or ignore you. Instead, while you were still a sinner, Jesus got up under the consequences and complications of your sin. And before He died, He said to go into the world and love one another as I have loved you." Why? It's because that's how you restore. Restoration happens when I'm willing to take on the consequences and complications caused by the sin of the person who's hurt me. I get up under the consequences and complications of their sin. But do you know why we can't do that? It's because we're so ticked off, hurt and angry. It's because the offense against us has dredged up all of this fear and insecurity in our own lives, and so we are dealing with our own tangled web of emotions. So, Paul says to us, "If you don't deal with the crud that comes to the surface in your life, when you respond to this person, you're going to push them further away and further into their sin and you'll never restore them. You won't grow; they won't grow, and it will just be a big mess."

Restoration isn't going to happen by sitting around and studying the Bible. It's not going to happen by drawing a hard line and giving ultimatums. It's not going to happen by having a twelve-step program or an accountability partner. I know because I had several...and I lied straight to their faces. The only way it's going to happen is by being willing to take on the consequences and complications caused by their sin

And if that wasn't enough, Paul says in Galatians 6:3: "If anyone thinks they are something when they are not, they deceive themselves." Do you know what that means? It means that if there's anything that rises to the surface in you that says, "I'm not doing that, not after what they've done," Paul responds, "Then you're guilty of leading your own mind astray because you think you're better than that other person; it's because you've forgotten where you came from – and you've deceived yourself." Let me put it another way: Somewhere along the way, you've forgotten what Jesus did for you. Somewhere along the way you've convinced yourself that you're so spiritual that you're above it all. You're thinking things like, "I would never do that!" And as long as you feel and think that way, you're worthless to God in the ministry of restoration" Isn't that convicting?

By the way, if you still don't buy all of this, just remember that Jesus spent the majority of His time on earth going around and restoring people. Do you remember what Jesus said in Matthew 7:3-4: "Why do you look at the speck of sawdust in your brother's eye and pay no attention to the plank in your own eye? How can you say to your brother, 'Let me take the speck out of your eye,' when all the time there is a plank in your own eye?" But do you know how we interpret that? We interpret it as, "Mind your own business." But in reality, Jesus is saying the same thing that Paul says. Jesus is saying, "When you notice something in another person's eye, chances are it's going to remind you of something you have in your own eye. But the goal isn't to ignore what's in their eye. The goal is to take care of what's in your own eye so you can help them with what's in their eye." That's why Jesus concludes in Matthew 7:5: "...and then you will see clearly to remove the speck from your brother's eye." In other words, when someone sins and that sin dredges up pride, insecurity and fear in your own life, allow God to deal with it. And once you've dealt with those things, then get up under the burden of their sins and work toward restoration.

As we saw earlier, that's what Jesus did in John 8 with the woman that was caught in the act of adultery. He didn't condemn her. He simply spoke to the men who presented her and made the accusation, "If you've never sinned, go ahead and throw your rock." And He asks, "Where are the ones that condemn you?" And she responds, "They've headed out of town." And then Jesus said, "Neither do I condemn you; go and sin no more." He didn't judge her; he restored her.

That's what Jesus did with the Samaritan Woman at the well in John 4. The Jews hated the Samaritans and the Samaritans knew it. And when Jesus walked up to her, He knew her life was a mess. He knew that she had already had five husbands and she was living with a sixth. But Jesus didn't walk up and say, "Don't you know that the Law of Moses condemns your lifestyle?" Instead He walked up and asked her for a drink. But she noticed that He didn't have anything to draw water with, and she realized the implication, "He's going to drink after me?" That would be like you finding a homeless drunk and asking him for a swig off of his bottle. That's why the woman was like, "What? You want to drink after me?" And if you are familiar with the story, Jesus didn't judge her; He restored her.

By the way, isn't that what Jesus did with us? He looked

down at this sinful world and said, "What a mess?" And He asked the Father, "How can I help?" And the Father sent Him to this earth. And Jesus never once said during His earthly ministry, "Do you know what your sin is going to cost me?" He just wanted to help. And that's the first relational step toward restoration. I want to wrap up this chapter by leaving you with three questions to ask yourself when someone disappoints and hurts you.

1st: "What am I feeling?"

2nd: "Is what I'm feeling appropriate?" By the way, to be mad at somebody because they've sinned is an inappropriate feeling. An appropriate feeling is sorrow.

3rd: "How can I help?" And if you will allow God to work you through your anger and fear and insecurities, it will become clear what God wants you to do. It's not that complicated. And we have no control over how the other person will respond, but our responsibility is to be a restorer. That's what our friend needs. That's what our family member needs. That's what our fellow church member needs. That's what our coworker and classmate and neighbor needs. That's what we will all need at sometime in our lives. If we are followers of Jesus, that's where God is taking us.

Chapter 9

"You Want Me to Do What?"

Most of us, whether we grew up in church or not, are familiar with what has become known as the Golden Rule. But what you may not know is that the Golden Rule is actually a quote from Jesus. The quote is found in Luke 6:31: "Do to others as you would have them do to you." You probably remember the King James Version of that verse, "Do unto others as you would have them do unto you." And I'm guessing that this was probably one of the rules that your parents encouraged you to live by and you did your best to obey it. But eventually we all grow up and we leave home and when we do, we quickly come to the realization that it's a dog-eat-dog world and often we get caught wearing pork chop underwear. For example, when you got married you assumed that you were going to live happily-ever-after, but somewhere along the way, your spouse changed their position from, "I do," to "I don't." Maybe the child that you planned on bringing you a lifetime of joy has, instead, given you nothing but heartache and pain. Maybe a fellow employee that you trusted stabbed you in the back to get the position you thought was yours. Maybe a good neighbor became a dreaded enemy. Maybe a loyal friend became a betrayer. Maybe your dream became a nightmare. Life has a way of changing our perspective. It often makes us cynical. And somewhere along the way, the Golden Rule morphed from, "Do unto others as you would have them do unto you," into, "Do unto others as they deserve to be done unto," or, "Do unto others before they do unto you." But we're learning in this book that, as Christians,

God has given us a brand new lens through which to view our relationships. Jesus said, "Do to others as I have done to you." A paraphrase could be, "Treat people the way that I've treated you." Do you know what Jesus was really saying? He was saying, "As I have unconditionally forgiven you, you are now to unconditionally forgive one another," to which we respond, "But they're not very forgivable!" To which Jesus responds, "And neither were you." To which we respond, "Oh, that's right."

But Jesus doesn't stop there. He goes on to say, "While you're at it, I also want you to love and accept each other as I have loved and accepted you." And if that's not enough to spend a lifetime trying to get right, in this chapter we're going to learn that, not only have we been called to love and forgive and accept each other, we've also been called upon to mutually (and here is the dreaded "S" word) submit to each other.

And this is a scary word, especially for women, and it's mainly because men have abused this word so much. In fact, for a lot of you men, you're not even sure where the verse is, but you are pretty sure there's a verse somewhere in the Bible about wives submitting to their husbands. By the way, I like to remind husbands that the first word in the verse is "wives," and they're like, "What's your point?" And I tell them, "It was written to wives, not you…mind your own business." But before we even get to that verse, the Apostle Paul gives us the bigger picture in Ephesians 5:21: "Submit to (who?) one another." And the word, submit, simply means, "to place yourself under someone's authority; to submit yourself to…" In other words, I'm to submit myself to your authority and you are to submit yourself to my authority. I'm to put you first and you are to put me first. That's what mutual submission looks like.

But the problem with submitting to one another is that we don't really want to do that. Our attitude is, "I want to be the boss and I want you to submit to me, after all, I'm right!" Isn't that the way we feel? We feel like, "If people were more like me, the world would be a better place." After all, don't we all see ourselves as the balanced ones? And to submit may mean that we have to admit that we're not right about something. As a result, I don't want to submit to you and you don't want to submit to me. And when you think about submitting to your family, it just sends chills up and down your spine. You're thinking, "If I were to submit to my family and put them before me, I would totally be taken advantage of; they would walk all over me."

In fact, some of you are already rejecting this whole idea of submitting because you have already tried it. You got married and you tried to put your spouse first, but you ended up leaving the marriage because you did all of the submitting and they did all of the dictating. You tried to serve them and put them first, and they were like, "Thanks," and they just let you do it, and eventually it just wore you out. And so, based on the fact that we're all inherently selfish, and based on the fact that some of us have tried this, there's something in us that says, "Thanks God, but I'll pass on the submitting stuff; what else you got, because I've tried it and it doesn't work."

And that's why the second half of Ephesians 5:21 is so powerful. Once again, Paul rips our attention off of the people around us and focuses us on why we're to submit to each other. In Ephesians 5:21 he says we're to submit to one another out of reverence (for the people in your life? – no) for Christ. So, Paul says, "I'm not asking you to submit to one another because one another is worth submitting too; I'm asking you to submit to one another because it shows reverence and respect for your Savior, Jesus Christ." In other words, if I put you first when you don't deserve to be put first, or you put me first when I don't deserve to be put first, it reflects on our reverence for what Jesus did for us 2,000 years ago on the cross. And Paul tells us that this should be the habit of our lives. It should always be, "others first" when it comes to our relationships. And it's not because the other person deserves it or because we might get something out of it.

We do it out of reverence for our Savior, Jesus Christ. And I know what you're thinking when you hear that. You're thinking, "If you knew my story, I'd get a pass!" And it's because we look at our relationships with all of their dysfunction and we think, "You've got to be kidding." But God says, "I'm not asking you to submit out of reverence for the irreverent people in your life. I'm asking you to do it out of reverence to Christ."

But here's the big question: What's the connection between reverence for Christ and submission to other people? Thankfully, in the Book of Philippians, Paul tells us what it looks like to submit to one another, and more importantly, he gives us some incredible insight into the significance of what Christ did for us. He shows us how Jesus actually submitted Himself to everyone who has ever lived. He shows us how Jesus put the needs and desires of everyone else ahead of his own, and now Jesus says, "Since I did that for you, I want you to do that for one another."

Now, the Book of Philippians is a letter that was written to a group of people in the city of Philippi. And Paul knew that these people experienced some of the same relationship struggles that we sometimes experience, and so he had a lot to say about the topic. And Paul begins Philippians 2 with a very unrealistic request and then he explains why he says it. Philippians 2:3 says: "Do nothing out of selfish ambition or vain conceit. Rather, in humility value others above yourselves." That means that you treat your spouse better than you treat yourself. You treat your parents better than you treat yourself. You treat your kids better than you treat yourself. You treat your neighbors better than you treat yourself. You treat your coworkers better than you treat yourself, and I think you are getting the point. You treat everyone in your life better than you treat yourself. And I know that some of you are thinking, "I'm not so sure," but that's what it means to submit. It means that you treat people as if they're better than you. Now, that doesn't mean that they are necessarily better than you, but you're to treat them as if they are.

And Paul continues in Philippians 2:4: "Not looking to your own interests but each of you to the interests of the others." And, again, that's a picture of what it means to submit to one another. But when we hear that, our minds automatically apply the brakes. We're like, "I just can't do that; I can't live that way; it won't work. It won't make me happy; nothing good is going to come from it." But then Paul connects us to the "why" behind this command in Philippians 2:5: "In your relationships with one another, have the same mindset as Christ Jesus." In the Greek text, this is a command; it literally says, "Have the same attitude and perspective as Christ Jesus."

And then Paul gives us a description of what Jesus' attitude was like in Philippians 2:6: "Who, being in very nature, God, did not consider equality with God something to be used to his own advantage." Do you know what that means? It means that when Jesus was on this earth, He never pulled rank. He never said. "I'm God and you're not, so just do what I say." He didn't go to Disney with the disciples and expect to get moved to the front of the line. He didn't act like a VIP. He didn't automatically expect the best table at His favorite restaurant. In other words, He didn't go around flashing His God card. Jesus never did that. He took his position and rank as God and He set it aside. And even though He outranked everybody, He never leveraged it for his own good. His attitude was, "I've got the position and the rank, but I'll just keep those things in my back pocket because that's secondary to your needs." And Paul says, "That's the attitude that you, as a Christian, should have."

And then Paul continues in Philippians 2:7: "Rather, He made himself nothing by taking the very nature of a servant, being made in human likeness." So, not only did He set aside his rank, He also set aside his rights. In fact, the gospels tell us that when Jesus came to this earth, He came as a servant, and He leveraged all of His power, not for His own sake, but for the sake of those that God had put in his life.

By the way, are you in a position where you have power over people? Are you a parent or a boss or a manager? Are you somebody that people look up to because of your position? Who do you leverage that position for? Most of us, left to ourselves, leverage it for ourselves. And then once our needs are met, we might leverage it for the people around us, especially if it involves a possible tax write-off. But when Jesus showed up on this earth, He had the right to anything He desired, but He put His rights on the back burner and leveraged His power for others. He became a servant. And Paul says, "Out of reverence for the one who did that for you, I want you to get into the habit of doing that for others. I want you to get into the habit of leveraging your rank and rights and power for the sake of the ones around you instead of for yourself." That's what it means to submit to one another.

And then Paul answers the big question that we are all wondering about: How far do you take this? You can see the answer in Philippians 2:8: "And being found in appearance as a man, he humbled himself by becoming obedient to death — even death on a cross!" Do you know what it means when it says that Jesus humbled himself? It means that Jesus placed Himself under people. It means that the Son of God allowed some smelly Roman soldier to manhandle Him. It means that the Son of God allowed people to spit on Him and to verbally abuse Him. It means that the Son of God allowed Himself to be nailed to a cross for the sake of someone else, and He never once demanded the respect he deserved. That's how far Jesus took this whole idea of putting other people ahead of Himself. Rank wasn't an issue. Rights weren't an issue. Respect wasn't an issue. He took the issues of rank and rights and respect and He set it all aside. And now He says to us, "Out of respect for me and for what I've done on your behalf, I want you to submit to one another." And our immediate response is, "But how far do I take it?" And I think Jesus' response is, "You'll have to figure that out for yourself, but let me tell you how far I took it: I took it to the point of death, even death on a cross."

It was almost as if Jesus had a dilemma. When He came to this earth, He could pull rank and demand His rights and He could get everything he deserved, or He could enter into a relationship with mankind, but He couldn't have it both ways. Because if Jesus had held onto His rank and rights and respect, He would have never died. And if He had never died, there would have been no sacrifice for our sins and there would have been no way for us to be invited into a relationship with God. So, it was either what He deserved or a relationship, and He left us a pattern to follow and it's this: Relationship takes precedence over our rank, our rights and the respect we think we deserve. It's the dilemma He faced and answered once and for all; and it's the dilemma we face everyday. Are we willing to sacrifice our rights and respect and rank for a relationship with the people God has placed in our lives? Jesus says, "I want you to do that, not because it works; not because you benefit from it; I want you to do it out of reverence and respect for me. And every time you put that other person first, it's a statement of the gratitude you have for me, and it's because I put you first and I put your needs ahead of my own."

And it's hard for us to wrap our brains around this, but Jesus also died for the sins of the person that drives you crazy. He died for the continuing sins of your spouse and your parents and your kids and your boss and your coworker and your neighbor and your roommate and your ex. He died for all the people that get on your last nerve, and Jesus understands that because I'm sure there are times when we still get on His last nerve. And so Jesus says, "I'm not asking for you to submit to them because they're worth submitting to; I'm asking you to submit to them out of reverence and respect for me. And just as I placed their needs ahead of my own needs when I died for their sins, I'm simply asking you to go as far as you can go without losing your mind or putting yourself in danger to submit to one another out of reverence and respect for me. And when you do that, you're giving me major-league gratitude for what I did for you." Question: If we lived that way, what would it do in our relationships? What would it do to you? What would it do to me? What would happen inside of us?

But the most amazing part of this passage is in Philippians 2:9-11: "Therefore God exalted him to the highest place and gave him the name that is above every name, that at the name of Jesus every knee should bow of those who are in heaven and on earth and under the earth, and every tongue acknowledge that Jesus Christ is Lord." Now let me give you a little theological quiz: Has every knee bowed to JC (yes or no)? Has every tongue acknowledged that Jesus Christ is Lord (yes or no)? The answer to both of those questions is a resounding, "No!" Why hasn't it happened yet? It's because our Savior continues to wait to get what He deserves, for the sake of those He still doesn't have a relationship with.

And I know that this sounds strange if you're not a Christian, but this is one of those weird things Christians believe. And we believe it because when a guy rises from the dead, we just believe Him. This is what Jesus said: "One day I'm going to come back to this earth and the whole world will know that I'm back." And that used to bother me until we got drones and satellites and CNN and cell phones, and so it's easier to believe now because we have the technology, and we'll all watch it while it's happening. And when Jesus returns, every knee will bow and every tongue will confess that Jesus Christ is who He said He is, and everyone will fall to the ground and acknowledge who He is. The reaction will be like blinking when an object zooms toward your eye. You won't be able to stop yourself; it will be that immediate and incredible. People will be like, "I thought Mike was kidding, but he was serious!"

But do you know why He's yet to show up to get the glory he deserves? It's because He knows that when He shows up for the second time, it's all over. He knows that mankind is going to lose the opportunity to follow Him. He knows that everyone is going to drop to his or her knees and proclaim that Jesus really is the Son of God, but at that point, nobody gets to choose anymore.

And so the reason that Jesus is still waiting to return and the reason that Jesus still hasn't received the respect and honor He deserves is because He continues to put the potential to have a relationship with mankind over what He deserves. It's because He knows that the day He returns and receives the glory, respect and honor that's due Him, there will be people with whom He has no relationship. And so, for the sake of a potential relationship with all mankind, Jesus continues to put His rights on hold. And while He continues to wait, Jesus says, "Mike, I want you to submit to the people around you; I want you to put others first. And when you do, it shows incredible reverence and respect for me."

Can you imagine what your family would look like if everyone mutually submitted? Can you imagine what your marriage would look like if both parties mutually submitted? Can you imagine what a church would like if everyone understood mutual submission. God says, "If you're waiting on the other person, you'll never do it, and so I'm asking you to go first. I'm asking you to submit, not out of reverence to them. I'm asking you to do it out of reverence for your Savior who put you first."

And I'm not smart enough to tell you how this works out in every scenario. I'm not smart enough to tell you how far to take it in your relationships, but here's the goal: Submit to one another out of reverence for your Savior who submitted on your behalf. Place the needs of others ahead of your own. And when we live that way, it's an incredible statement of our understanding of what Jesus has done for us and it will actually revolutionize how we love and accept and forgive and restore one another.

And I know that this is so much easier to write about than it is to actually do. I know that there are some spouses reading this who are thinking, "There's no way; I'm not going first." There are some parents or kids thinking, "There's no way; I'm not going first." If you're feeling that way, I encourage you to at least be willing to say, "Heavenly Father, in your grace and in your mercy, would you give me the courage to decide: 'Out of reverence for what Jesus did for me, I'm submitting. Even if I don't get anything out of this, I'm submitting.'" For those of you that work for unreasonable bosses and the last thing you want to do is to submit to that person, I pray that God will give you a glimpse of what it would look like to go into the office with an attitude that says, "This isn't about where I work or who I work for. Out of reverence for my Savior, I'm going to submit." It will take courage, but how would all of our relationships change if we just decided to submit to one another? How would restoration of the broken and downcast look if there was no hierarchy? What if it was just two sinners, both saved by grace, mutually submitting to one another? A man can dream...

Chapter 10

"You're Saying There's a Chance!"

When we think of Jesus, we often think of Him as kind and loving and gentle and accepting, and all of those things are true. But Jesus was also the most revolutionary person that's ever lived. And if you don't agree with my assessment, just think about how He lived. He wasn't born into royalty; He was born in obscurity. He was raised in the military village of Nazareth. He worked with His hands for thirty years. He wasn't considered an intellectual by anyone in His day. When He launched His ministry, He chose callused fisherman and a crooked tax gatherer for His companions. He chastised the "good" people who turned the temple into a marketplace, but as we earlier saw, He publicly defended an adulteress and rescued her from stoning. He angrily denounced the Pharisees as blind guides, hypocrites and fools, and He refused to play by their pious rules. He preferred hanging out with genuine, garden variety, up front, lost people with no intentions of impressing anybody.

How about what He taught; talk about revolutionary! In a society ruled by legalistic rules and regulations, He said, "Don't judge." In a world dying with anxiety, He said, "Don't worry." In a day when showing off was an art form, He said, "When you pray, do it in private. When you give, don't toot a horn. When you fast, don't look like you have a stomach bug. Instead of hating, forgive your enemy. Instead of intimidating, serve." And although the Prophet Isaiah said that Jesus would be like a Lamb led to the slaughter, which ended up being true, as we wrap up this book we are going to see why Jesus was the greatest leader that ever lived and why he was so worthy to be followed. It doesn't matter where you've been or what you've done. As Corrie Ten Boom said, "There is no pit so deep, that God's love is not deeper still." If you are willing to follow, He will lead you.

To help you see that truth, I want to begin by looking at one of the coolest scenes in all the gospels. Let's pick up the story in John 21:1-14: "Afterward Jesus appeared again to his disciples, by the Sea of Galilee. It happened this way: Simon Peter, Thomas (also known as Didymus), Nathanael from Cana in Galilee, the sons of Zebedee, and two other disciples were together. 'I'm going out to fish,' Simon Peter told them, and they said, 'We'll go with you.' So, they went out and got into the boat, but that night they caught nothing. Early in the morning, Jesus stood on the shore, but the disciples did not realize that it was Jesus. He called out to them, 'Friends, haven't you any fish?' 'No,' they answered. He said, 'Throw your net on the right side of the boat and you will find some.' When they did, they were unable to haul in the net because of the large number of fish. Then the disciple whom Jesus loved said to Peter, 'It is the Lord!' As soon as Simon Peter heard Him say, 'It is the Lord,' he wrapped his outer garment around him (for he had taken it off) and jumped into the water. The other disciples followed in the boat, towing the net full of fish, for they were not far from shore, about a hundred yards. When they landed, they saw a fire of burning coals there with fish on it, and some bread. Jesus said to them, 'Bring some of the fish you have just caught.' So Simon Peter climbed back into the boat and dragged the net ashore. It was full of large fish, 153, but even with so many the net was not torn. Jesus said to them, 'Come and have breakfast.' None of the disciples dared ask Him, 'Who are you?' They knew it was the Lord. Jesus came, took the bread and gave it to them, and did the same with the fish. This was now the third time Jesus appeared to his disciples after he was raised from the dead."

And I always wonder if Peter's stomach knotted up when

you get to John 21:15: "When they had finished eating, Jesus said to Simon Peter, 'Simon son of John, do you love me more than these?'" And the word translated love is the Greek word, agape. We talked about this word a lot when we unpacked 1 Corinthians 13 earlier in Chapter 5. It's the highest form of love you can have for an individual. It's seeking the highest good of another person. It's putting that person's needs above your own needs. And Jesus asks Peter, "Do you love me with that kind of love?" And Peter responds in John 21:15, "'Yes, Lord,' he said, 'you know that I love you.'" But when Peter responds, he doesn't use the Greek word, agape. Peter uses another Greek word for love. He uses the word, *phileo*. It means, fond affection. Sometimes it's translated, brotherly love. Peter responds, "I wish I could say that I have the highest form of love for you, but the best I can say is that I have a fond affection for you." But even though that was Peter's response, Jesus replies in John 21:15-16: "Feed my lambs." Again Jesus said, "Simon son of John, do you love me?" And once again, Jesus uses the word, agape, that highest form of love. And Peter answers, "Yes, Lord, you know that I love you." And for the second time, Peter answers Jesus question by using the word, *phileo*. In other words, "Yes, Lord, I have a fond affection for you." And Jesus once again responds in John 21:16: "Take care of my sheep." John 21:17 continues: "The third time he said to him, 'Simon son of John, do you love me?'" But this time, Jesus switches things up and throws Peter a curve ball and Jesus uses the Greek word for love, *phileo*. In other words, Jesus asks, "Peter, is the best you can say is that you have a fond affection for me?" John 21:17 tells us, Peter was hurt because Jesus asked him the third time, "Do you love (phileo) me?" So Jesus asks Peter, "Is the best you can do is say that you have a fond affection for me?" And Peter answered in John 21:17: "Lord, you know all things…" In other words, "Jesus, let's keep it real. You know what I'm like. You know my background. You know my nature. You know how I denied three times that I even knew you. No more bold proclamations. No more statements like, 'I'll die for you!' You know that the best I can say is that I'm fond of you." And I'm sure that Peter began to pick up his things to leave because he was prepared for Jesus to say, "You're done! You're out of the group! You're either all in or you're out! There's no room here for mediocre disciples." But to Peter's amazement, Jesus said in John 21:17: "Feed my sheep." Jesus doesn't put Peter on probation until he can prove that he can be trusted or that he can change his evil ways. Jesus simply responds to Peter, "Even if the best you can say is that you have a fond affection for me, I can still use you. You have value to me. Let's get back to work."

This is a great lesson for all of us: Past failures don't disqualify us from doing great things for God. I want you to let that sink in. I'm sure that Peter's thinking was no different than ours: "In order to be used, I've got to earn the right to be used." In other words, we believe that we either need to be perfect or as near perfect as possible for God to be able to use us. And we think that way because that's the way it works in the world in which we live. And it's because, from the time we're born we're taught that if we're going to succeed in life, we have to perform at a top level and so we work hard and long at getting a job done. We rely on our competence, training, or experience. We put together the right procedures. We make sure that we give 100% in accomplishing the task. And there's nothing wrong with any of those things, but what happens when we do all of those things and we still fail? There's that sense of remorse and guilt.

And it's in the midst of those kinds of emotions that Jesus asks Peter, "Do you love me?" But I can guarantee you that, by this point, Peter had long since given up on the possibility of ever doing anything significant. In his mind he was a loser and a failure. He had a lower approval rating than Joe Biden. He hadn't come through when the chips were down and he planned on returning to what he knew, fishing.

Do you ever feel like that? Sure you do. But there's hardly a man or woman in the Bible used greatly by God who didn't fail greatly. In fact, you're in pretty good company when you screw up. Abraham lied about Sarah not being his wife and ended up being the Father of the Jewish nation. Moses was a murderer and he ended being the deliverer. David committed adultery with Bathsheba and then had her husband knocked off, but yet he was still considered, "a man after God's own heart." Jonah did the opposite of what God wanted him to do and ended up in the belly of a great fish, but then preached a message in Nineveh that turned the people's hearts toward God. Peter denied that even knew who Jesus was, only to stand on a street corner in Jerusalem a few weeks later and deliver a sermon and three thousand people began to follow Jesus. It almost makes you want to really screw up when you hear a list like that.

Who ever came up with the idea that you have to be perfect to be used by God? I sure wouldn't have ever been a pastor. Most churches wouldn't have much of a staff. The mission fields around the world would be void of missionaries. Ministries like Campus Crusade and Young Life would become extinct. But the amazing thing about God's grace is that His love covers a multitude of sins and failures and screw-ups. In fact, when I'm at my worst, God is at His best. Think about this: David has the affair with Bathsheba and then he has her husband killed to cover it all up. But did you know that David and Bathsheba, the couple that committed adultery, were blessed with a son; his name was Solomon. And it was Solomon, the product of an adulterous and murderous relationship, not David, the man after God's own heart, who was allowed to build God's temple! And as a bonus, God also made sure that Solomon was the wisest man that ever lived. You can't make this stuff up. That's grace. When we are at our worst, God is at His best.

Recently the Winter Olympics were taking place and there was a night during the games when I was suffering from a bout of insomnia. No matter what I tried, I could not go to sleep. So, I turned on the Olympics and the event that was airing was couples' ice skating. The timing could not have been more perfect because, not only can couples' ice skating put me to sleep, it can send me right into a coma. I mean, couples' ice skating makes golf look like an MMA event.

Well, on this particular night the crowd was very subdued as a couple performed their routine. Eventually, after what seemed like hours but was probably only forty-five seconds, the couple came to the point in the routine where the guy was to launch the girl into the air to do some kind of triple something, something and I witnessed something I had never seen before. Not only did the girl miss her landing and go sliding across the ice, the guy lost his balance after throwing his date and did a face plant. Like the true professionals they were, they quickly regained their composure and set off to complete the event, but it was the crowd that caught my attention. After this huge failure on the part of these skaters who had prepared their entire lives for this moment, the crowd, which had been quiet and subdued, rose to its feet and cheered as loudly as I have ever heard a skating crowd cheer. And, all to encourage this couple that had just massively blown it to finish strong. My first thought was, "I wonder if that's what Heaven is like when we blow it?" Is it possible that it's in those tragic moments of failure in our lives that God stands alongside that great crowd of witnesses that the writer of Hebrews refers to, and they cheer us on louder than ever, encouraging us to get up and finish strong? When we are at our worst, God with His grace is at His best. No one can appreciate the grace of God more than the person who's blown it big time, and that's what Peter heard that day.

You may be reading this while living in the backwash of a terrible failure, but you can still do great things for God. In fact, the history of Christianity is littered with leaders who have a track record of failure. There wouldn't even be a Bible if it weren't for the people who failed miserably, but got up off of the ice to finish strong. Jesus said to Peter the third time, "Get up; feed my sheep; I can still use you." And by now, Peter must have been thinking, "Okay, I get it; but what is it that you want me to do? Do you want me to go back to school? Do you want me to relocate to a new area? Do you want me to sell all of my possessions and give the money to the poor? Just tell me what you want me to do because I'll do anything and I'll go anywhere! You've got me where you want me."

Notice what Jesus said in John 21:18-19: "'Very truly I tell you, when you were younger you dressed yourself and went where you wanted.'" (Jesus tells Peter that it won't always be that way.) "'But when you are old you will stretch out your hands, and someone else will dress you and lead you where you do not want to go.' Jesus said this to indicate the kind of death by which Peter would glorify God."

The Bible never tells us how Peter died, but historians do. Peter and his wife were imprisoned under Nero's rule in AD 61. One morning, Peter was forced to watch while his wife was executed. Afterwards, he was then taken back to his own cell where he stayed overnight. The next morning when they brought Peter to the place of his crucifixion, he said, "I'm not worthy to be crucified as my Lord," and he requested to be crucified upside down. He was led to where he did not wish to go. His hands were stretched out against his wishes, and he died nailed upside down on a cross. It's a moving picture, isn't it? It's Jesus' way of telling Peter, "The cost of following me will be high." But if Peter was to be used greatly, that's the lesson that Jesus needed him to learn.

By the way, this is a good time to remind all of us that there's definitely an upside to following Christ, but there are also some downsides. There's a great example of this in Luke 9:57: "As they were walking along the road, a man said to him, 'I will follow you wherever you go.'" I'm guessing that this guy had seen all this great stuff that Jesus had been doing. He witnessed Jesus forgiving people and showing mercy and healing the sick, and his reaction was, "Count me in. I'm not just a tire-kicker; I'm a buyer!" And Jesus decided to give this man a lesson on animals. Jesus said in Luke 9:58 (NLT): "Foxes have dens to live in, and birds have nests, but I, the Son of Man, have no home of my own, not even a place to lay my head." That's a little odd; why did Jesus say that? Well, He wasn't saying that He was dirt poor. He was saying, "I'm the Son of God; I'm the Messiah, and you'll notice that there's some serious sacrificing going on. So when you choose to follow Me, there's an upside, but there's also a downside, so you'd better realize what you're signing up for. If you follow Me, things are going to change," and that's true.

If you're a believer, think about your life before you became a Christ follower. For example, before Christ, your morality was pretty much based on your view of life and situation ethics. You thought things like, "I'm not going to be that bad, but I'm not going to be that good either; after all, boys will be boys; girls will be girls." But once you became a Christ follower, things changed. All of a sudden, you're sin-sensitive and the things that didn't bother you before begin to bother you. The Holy Spirit begins to tweak your conscience and you think things like, "Man, I shouldn't have said that; I shouldn't have thought that; I shouldn't have done that." That kind of stuff happens once you become a Christ follower. Not only that, your entire attitude about material possessions is changed and reoriented; it's just going to happen. Prior to becoming a Christ follower, your attitude was, "My stuff is my stuff and my money is my money. If I want to buy that house, I'll buy it. If I want that car, I'll get it. If I want to take that trip, I'll take it. It's my money and I'm going to do what I want to do with it." But once you decide to follow Jesus, you realize that you don't own a thing; you're just a manager. You're just a steward of what God has given you, and so your stuff isn't your stuff anymore. Actually, it never was, but now you realize it.

Following Jesus will impact your relationships. Once a single person steps over the line and says, "Jesus, I will follow you," do you know what the Bible says? It says that you're only to marry other Christ followers. So, as a Christian, suddenly two-thirds of the potential candidates for you to marry have been wiped out. My point is, there's going to be some changes. There are going to be some sacrifices and tough sledding along the way. Just like with Peter, our decision to follow Christ comes with a price.

John 21:19: "Then he said to him, 'Follow me!'" The Greek literally says, "Keep on following me." It means, "Start now and never stop." And there's no mention of geography or education or requirements. He just says, "Follow me now and keep on following me." And just so you know, this is the same command that Jesus still has for each one of us: "Follow me, and keep on following." If you fall, and we all do, get up and keep following.

Are you still thinking that you're not worthy to follow Jesus? Are you still believing the lie that your sin or failure was just too great to recover from? Is it that you're not lovely enough? Do you think that something in your past makes you unacceptable? Is that the problem? Some churches may see you that way. Certainly some Christians may see you that way. But I can assure you that your Heavenly Father doesn't see you that way. Let me give it one more shot; I saved the best for last.

Early on in this book we looked at some of the unsavory characters in Jesus' family tree. By the way, there's a definite lesson I've learned from studying the genealogy of Jesus: Digging into your heritage can be a gamble. I mean, it's one thing to find out that you're a descendant of Robert E. Lee, depending on what part of the country you're from. But it's another thing to discover that your third cousin twice removed is Jeffrey Dahmer. I mean, you'd probably keep that to yourself, because when we look into our family tree, we're hoping to find good people. But in our study, we've discovered that Matthew did something very odd when he laid out Jesus' family heritage because, not only does he underscore the great people like Abraham and Isaac and Jacob and David, he also highlights some of the sleazy relatives in Jesus' past. In fact, he underscored people that you would intentionally leave out of your family tree. And earlier on we addressed the question, "Why would Matthew do that?" It's because Matthew's message is that since the beginning of time, God has distributed His grace and mercy and forgiveness to people who didn't deserve it. And so the reason they're a part of the story is because they're the point of the story. By the way, it's also the reason that we're the point of the story. In spite of what we have or haven't done, God distributes His grace and mercy and forgiveness to us. That's the gospel in a nutshell.

And so Matthew wrote in Matthew 1:1-5: "This is the genealogy of Jesus the Messiah the son of David, the son of Abraham: Abraham was the father of Isaac, Isaac the father of Jacob, Jacob the father of Judah and his brothers, Judah the father of Perez and Zerah, whose mother was Tamar, Perez the father of Hezron, Hezron the father of Ram, Ram the father of Amminadab, Amminadab the father of Nahshon, Nahshon the father of Salmon, Salmon the father of Boaz, whose mother was Rahab…" And I can guarantee you that this Jewish audience cringed when Matthew got to the name, Rahab, and it's because, as we learned already, Rahab had a nickname. By the way, she's not the only person in the Bible with a nickname. There's John the Baptist. There's Uriah the Hittite. There's Simon the Sorcerer. There's Jabba the Hut. Actually, he's not in the Bible, but Jabba is from the Hebrew word for frog. My point is, it's not uncommon for people to have a nickname to describe them. Unfortunately for Rahab, she was known as Rahab the harlot. Not only that, Rahab wasn't Jewish, she was Canaanite, which means that she was the enemy of the Jews. And this creates some tension in the genealogy of Jesus, because now we have a harlot right in the middle of the lineage of Jesus, which brings up the question: Why would Matthew include her in the story? It's because, not only is she part of the story; she's the point of the story. So, let me tell you about Rahab the harlot.

When we pick up the story, Israel has just become a brand new nation. After 430 years of slavery and another 40 years wandering around the desert, they've finally make it to the Promised Land. By the way, this is the land that Abraham, Isaac, Jacob and Joseph lived in before the Jews ended up in Egypt looking for grain. When you think about it, they're really going back home. But now, instead of a few family members, there are about 2.5 million Jews making their way into the Promised Land. And just as God instructed, they cross the Jordan River and they begin to run the inhabitants out of the land so they can retake the land that God had promised them.

But in the process of taking the land, they come up against the city of Jericho. And so Joshua sends a couple of spies into Jericho to find out what they're up against. And as the two spies are scouting out the city, someone spots them, and the men who spot them go and report it to the king and so the king sends out an order to find them. And so the army of Jericho begins to search for these two men, and someone spots these guys ducking into a house. And the house happens to belong to a woman whose name is Rahab, and she happens to be a prostitute.

And we're not told why, but instead of barging into Rahab's house, the guards just knock on the door. My guess is, you don't want to barge into a prostitute's home because you never know who you might stumble across. And so they knock on the door and say to Rahab, "Someone said they saw a couple of Hebrew dudes going into your home; have you seen them?" And Rahab lies and says, "They were here, but they left right before sundown, right before the gates of the city were locked. In fact, if you take off now, you might still catch them." And so the guards leave and they continue to search for these two spies, and then Rahab goes back into the house and has a conversation with these guys.

Let's pick up the story in Joshua 2:8-11: "Before the spies lay down for the night, she went up on the roof and said to them, 'I know that the Lord (the Hebrew word used here is for the highest name for God; it mean "the existing One") has given you this land and that a great fear of you has fallen on us, so that all who live in this country are melting in fear because of you. We have heard how the Lord dried up the water of the Red Sea for you when you came out of Egypt, and what you did to Sihon and Og, the two kings of the Amorites east of the Jordan River, whom you completely destroyed. When we heard of it, our hearts melted in fear and everyone's courage failed because of you, for the Lord your God is the God in heaven above and on the earth below.'"

So, Rahab says, "In spite of what I've been taught, I believe that your God can beat up my God. I believe that your God, whoever your God is, is THE God who reigns and rules over any god I have in my belief system."

Joshua 2:12-15: "'Now then, please swear to me by the Lord that you will show kindness to my family, because I have shown kindness to you. Give me a sure sign that you will spare the lives of my father and mother, my brothers and sisters, and all who belong to them—and that you will save us from death.'" 'Our lives for your lives!' the men assured her. If you don't tell what we are doing, we will treat you kindly and faithfully when the Lord gives us the land.'" So, she let them down by a rope through the window, for the house she lived in was part of the city wall.

And these guys eventually make their way back to Joshua, and they tell him about their clandestine experience. And they report to Joshua, "Everyone in the city of Jericho is scared to death. In fact, they may just open the gate and surrender." And

if you've been around church for a while, you're probably familiar with the next part of the story; it's the story of the Battle of
Jericho. God tells the Hebrew people to march around the city
of Jericho once a day for six straight days, and then to walk
around the city walls seven times on the seventh day. And after
they completed the final lap on the final day, they were to shout
at the top of their lungs and the priest were to blow their horns
and the walls would fall down. And the people obeyed, and it
happens just as God said. By the way, the reason for this strange
strategy was so that God would get credit for the victory and
everybody in the surrounding nations would know that you
don't mess with Israel's God. But when the walls collapsed, it
was pure chaos. The people of Jericho are paralyzed with fear
as the people of Israel rush in and take the city. And in the midst
of all of this chaos and terror and bloodshed, God spares one
family because of the faith of a Canaanite hooker. And this is
how the story concludes in Joshua 6:22, 25: "Joshua said to the
two men who had spied out the land, 'Go into the prostitute's
house and bring her out and all who belong to her, in accordance
with your oath to her.' But Joshua spared Rahab the prostitute,
with her family and all who belonged to her, because she hid the
men Joshua had sent as spies to Jericho—and she lives among
the Israelites to this day." In other words, Rahab lived among
the Israelites as a reminder of something that was foreign to their
way of thinking, and it was this: "Israel's God is a God of grace
and mercy and forgiveness, so much so, that He spared an
enemy. In fact, Israel's God is a God who would even spare a
prostitute, who, by His own Law, should have been stoned to
death."

   But that's not the end of the story because a few years later,
a man named Salmon walked up to Rahab and said, "Hey,
maybe we can grab a cup of coffee or go to a movie sometime."
And then later on, maybe they went to dinner at Ruth Chris'.
And one thing leads to another and they fall in love and this

Jewish man marries this Canaanite woman. And they have a baby boy and they name him Boaz (I don't know why, but that's what they named him). And when Boaz became an adult, he was introduced to a young woman named Ruth, the Moabite. And they get married and they have a baby, and Boaz and Ruth's great grandson is King David himself.

And Matthew brings all of this to the attention of his readers because he knew that the story of Rahab illustrates the entire story and message of the gospel. I mean, here's a woman that was condemned by the Law of Moses. She was an outsider, an enemy and a lawbreaker in a time when life was ruled by the Law. And God says, "In spite of My Law, My grace, mercy and forgiveness trumps My Law and My judgment. In fact, My grace, mercy and forgiveness is so broad, not only can I forgive Rahab and save her life, I can also incorporate her into the lineage of Jesus, the Messiah."

It's an absolutely incredible story – and it's THE perfect illustration of why I wrote this book because I don't think Rahab's story is that much different than our story. Because, just as she had a nickname, Rahab the harlot, I think that probably all of us have a nickname, don't we? Some of you have nicknames that have recently been discovered. It may be why you are reading this book. Some of you have nicknames that you've tried to put behind you, but every once-in-a-while you run into someone from high school, or college, or a previous job and you're reminded that, in their mind, you have a nickname. You just can't seem to shake it. For some of you, you have a nickname in the mind of your ex-spouse, and so you wish you could go back and undo what you've done but you can't go back and undo it. And it's really easy for us to look down our noses at someone like Rahab the harlot, but the truth is, her story is our story. Because, like Rahab, when you think about following Jesus, the first thing that comes to your mind is your nickname. And so you back off and think, "God would never take me seriously; why even try.

I have a nickname; I have a reputation."

I actually made a list of some nicknames (maybe one describes you)

Kerry the Coveter

Gretchen the Greedy

Gail the Gossip

Allan the Addict

Sally the Slanderer

Larry the Luster

Don the Deceiver

Gale the Glutton

Drake the Drunk

Jason the Jealous

Thelma the Thief

Charlie the Cheater

Paul the Proud

Mike the Adulterer

Like it or not, we all have a nickname, including myself. And so when Matthew got to this point in the genealogy, he threw in Rahab the harlot. And maybe it's because Matthew had a nickname as well, Matthew the Tax Collector. And as we saw earlier, one day Jesus walked up and looked at Matthew the Tax Collector, but Jesus didn't say, "Once you quit being a tax collector, feel free to follow me." Or, "Once you repent and promise to never do it again, follow me." Or, "Once you get your act together and get a new reputation, follow me." That's not what Jesus said. Matthew remembered Jesus walking up and looking him in the eyes and saying, "Matthew, I want you to follow me."

The same Jesus invited all kinds of people with all kinds of nicknames to follow Him while they still had their nickname, and it's because Jesus' righteousness didn't overshadow His mercy. His holiness didn't overshadow His grace and forgiveness, regardless of the nickname.

And so, Rahab the harlot is the Great, Great, Great, Great,

Great, Great, ,Great, Great Grandmother of Jesus, the Messiah. And that's the point of the story. Isn't that powerful; and doesn't it make you want to re-think your approach to God? Doesn't that make you want to change how you view and judge yourself? Doesn't that make you want to change how you view and judge others? Because the message of the gospel is that God has done for us what we could not do for ourselves. And regardless of the nickname you have or the reputation that follows you, just like me, you've been invited to have a relationship with the God who longs to have a relationship with you. You don't have to wait until you clean up your act. You don't have to wait until you get it all together. You are invited into a relationship with God now. Just like Peter and just like Rahab, you're invited to follow Him now. And that's the gospel story. God decided to pay for the sins of all mankind, once and for all, and He decided to invite us into a relationship with Him. And once that relationship is begun, He'll begin to chip away at all the things we don't want in our lives anyway. But that's not in order to begin the relationship; it's a result of being in the relationship.

When I was 18 years old, I chose as my life verse Galatians 2:20: "I have been crucified with Christ and I no longer live, but Christ lives in me. The life I now live in the body, I live by faith in the Son of God, who loved me and gave himself for me." After my moral collapse, I decided that it was time for a new life verse. I chose a verse that we looked at earlier. It's the words of Paul from Philippians 3:13-14: "Brothers and sisters, I do not consider myself yet to have taken hold of it. But one thing I do: Forgetting what is behind and straining toward what is ahead, I press on toward the goal to win the prize for which God has called me heavenward in Christ Jesus." And as I press on, I continue to fol-low...and there are days that I fall...but I get back up and continue following.

Whatever your story may be, whatever your past may hold, I want to encourage you to do the same. Ignore the haters and the naysayers. Just like Jesus said of the poor, they will always be with us. Get back up, brush yourself off, and resume following. The old dream may be dead, but a new one is just around the bend. It's the only life worth living. It's like one of my favorite writings I've ever come across. It's from Tim Hansel's book entitled, Holy Sweat.

"At first, I saw God as my observer, my judge, keeping track of the things I did wrong, so as to know whether I merited heaven or hell when I die. He was out there sort of like a president. I recognized His picture when I saw it, but I really didn't know Him.

But later on when I met Christ, it seemed as though life was rather like a bike ride, but it was a tandem bike, and I noticed that Christ was in the back helping me pedal. I don't know just when it was that He suggested we change places, but life has not been the same since.

When I had control, I knew the way. It was rather boring, but predictable . . . It was the shortest distance between two points. But when He took the lead, He knew delightful long cuts, up mountains, and through rocky places at breakneck speeds, it was all I could do to hang on! Even though it looked like madness, He said, "Pedal!"

I worried and was anxious and asked, "Where are you taking me?" He laughed and didn't answer, and I started to learn to trust. I forgot my boring life and entered into the adventure. And when I'd say, "I'm scared," He'd lean back and touch my hand. He took me to people with gifts that I needed, gifts of healing, acceptance and joy. They gave me gifts to take on my journey, my Lord's and mine. And we were off again. He said, "Give the gifts away; they are extra baggage, too much weight." So, I did, to the people we met, and I found that in giving I received, and still our burden was light.

I did not trust Him, at first, in control of my life. I thought He'd wreck it; but He knows bike secrets, knows how to make it bend to take sharp corners, knows how to jump to clear high rocks, knows how to fly to shorten scary passages. And I am learning to shut up and pedal in the strangest places, and I'm beginning to enjoy the view and the cool breeze on my face with my delightful constant companion, Jesus Christ.

And when I'm sure I just can't do it anymore, He just smiles and says . . . 'Pedal.'"

— author unknown

About the Author

Mike Lee served as a lead pastor for over 40 years, teaching the Bible in dynamic, relevant and insightful ways. In 1994, he relocated from California to Raleigh, North Carolina along with four families to start Hope Community Church. During his 27 years of leadership at Hope, the congregation grew into one of the largest churches in America. Although Mike is now retired from the pastorate, he still continues to teach about the transformational power of God's word. He and his wife, Shannon currently reside in Apex, North Carolina.

ABOOKS

ALIVE Book Publishing and ALIVE Publishing Group
are imprints of Advanced Publishing LLC,
3200 A Danville Blvd., Suite 204, Alamo, California 94507

Telephone: 925.837.7303
alivebookpublishing.com

CPSIA information can be obtained
at www.ICGtesting.com
Printed in the USA
LVHW110154041222
734525LV00006BA/755

9 781631 321849